State of Qatar: Iran's Open Window to the World

Copyright Page

TITLE: State of Qatar: Iran's Open Window to the World

1ST Edition

Copyright @ 2023

Roberto M. Rodriguez. All rights reserved.

ISBN: 9798223920168

Table of Contents

STATE OF QATAR: IRAN'S OPEN WINDOW TO THE WORLD

By Roberto Miguel Rodriguez

Chapter 1: State of Qatar: Isolated Iran's Open Window to the World

The Geopolitical Landscape of the Gulf Region

As diplomats and representatives of various nations, it is crucial for us to understand the geopolitical landscape of the Gulf region, particularly in relation to the State of Qatar and its relationship with Iran. This subchapter titled "The Geopolitical Landscape of the Gulf Region" aims to provide a comprehensive overview of the political, economic, cultural, and strategic dynamics that shape this important region.

Qatar, often described as Iran's open window to the world, plays a significant role in the Gulf region's geopolitical landscape. Despite being geographically small, Qatar has emerged as a major player in diplomatic relations with Iran. Its unique position allows it to bridge the gap between Iran and the international community, fostering dialogue and understanding.

In terms of diplomatic relations, Qatar and Iran have maintained a cordial and mutually beneficial partnership. Both countries share common interests, including regional stability, counterterrorism efforts, and economic collaboration. Qatar's diplomatic efforts have played a pivotal role in easing tensions and fostering dialogue between Iran and other Gulf countries.

Furthermore, Qatar and Iran have developed strong trade and economic relations. Despite international sanctions on Iran, Qatar has continued to engage in trade with its Iranian counterparts, contributing to both nations' economic growth. This trade relationship extends beyond traditional sectors, with cooperation in areas such as tourism, cultural exchange, and academic collaboration.

Energy cooperation is another significant aspect of Qatar and Iran's relationship. Both countries are major players in the global energy market and have collaborated on several energy projects. This cooperation strengthens their respective positions and contributes to regional stability.

Political cooperation and alliances between Qatar and Iran also shape the geopolitical landscape of the Gulf region. Both countries have supported each other in regional conflicts and have worked together to address shared challenges. This cooperation has helped foster stability and security in the region.

Sports diplomacy, education and academic collaboration, transport and connectivity, security cooperation, and media and information exchange are other vital dimensions of Qatar and Iran's relationship. These diverse areas of collaboration further reinforce their strong ties and contribute to the overall stability and development of the Gulf region.

In conclusion, the geopolitical landscape of the Gulf region is heavily influenced by the relationship between Qatar and Iran. As diplomats, it is essential for us to recognize and understand the multifaceted nature of this relationship and its impact on the various niches, such as diplomatic relations, trade and economic cooperation, cultural exchange, energy collaboration, political alliances, sports diplomacy, education, transport, security, and media. By comprehending these dynamics, we can navigate the complexities of the Gulf region and work towards fostering peace, stability, and prosperity in this important part of the world.

Qatar's Strategic Position in the Middle East

In the ever-shifting landscape of the Middle East, Qatar has emerged as a key player, strategically positioned to bridge the gap between regional powers and facilitate diplomatic, economic, cultural, and political exchanges. This subchapter will delve into Qatar's unique role as a mediator and facilitator, addressing the various aspects of its strategic position in the region.

Qatar's strategic position as Iran's open window to the world has been instrumental in fostering diplomatic relations between the two nations. As isolated as Iran may be, Qatar has played a crucial role in maintaining channels of communication, allowing for dialogue and negotiations to take place. This has been vital in easing tensions and promoting stability in the region.

The diplomatic relations between Qatar and Iran have not only been limited to political discussions, but also extend to trade and economic cooperation. Qatar has become an important trading partner for Iran, facilitating bilateral trade and investment opportunities. Through its strategic location, Qatar has helped Iran access global markets, boosting their economy and opening up avenues for growth.

Cultural exchange and tourism have also flourished between Qatar and Iran. Qatar's commitment to promoting cultural understanding and appreciation has led to increased tourism between the two nations. Cultural events, exhibitions, and festivals have been held to showcase the rich heritage and traditions of both countries, fostering mutual understanding and respect.

Energy cooperation between Qatar and Iran has been a significant aspect of their strategic partnership. Qatar, being one of the world's largest producers of liquefied natural gas (LNG), has collaborated with Iran to develop energy projects, ensuring a stable supply of energy for both nations and the wider region.

Political cooperation and alliances have further solidified Qatar's strategic position in the Middle East. Qatar has actively engaged in regional initiatives and organizations, working closely with Iran to address common challenges and promote peace and stability in the region.

Sports diplomacy has also been a tool for Qatar and Iran to strengthen their ties. Through sports events and collaborations, they have fostered mutual respect and understanding, transcending political differences and promoting a sense of unity among their people.

Furthermore, Qatar and Iran have established strong educational and academic collaborations, facilitating the exchange of knowledge and expertise. This has led to the development of educational programs, research partnerships, and student exchanges, enriching the academic landscape of both countries.

Transport and connectivity have been enhanced between Qatar and Iran, with improved air, sea, and land links. This has facilitated the movement of goods, people, and ideas, further strengthening their economic and cultural ties.

Qatar's strategic position has also contributed to security cooperation between the two nations. Qatar and Iran have collaborated on intelligence sharing and counterterrorism efforts, working together to combat common threats in the region.

Lastly, media and information exchange have played a crucial role in Qatar's strategic position in the Middle East. Through media outlets and information sharing platforms, Qatar has provided a platform for open dialogue, promoting understanding and awareness among nations.

In conclusion, Qatar's strategic position in the Middle East as Iran's open window to the world has enabled the nation to play a pivotal role in various aspects, including diplomacy, trade, culture, energy, politics, sports, education, transport, security, and media. By leveraging its unique geographical location and fostering strong partnerships, Qatar has successfully bridged the gap between Iran and the world, contributing to regional stability and prosperity.

The Isolation of Iran and its Implications

In recent years, Iran has faced increasing isolation from the international community, with significant implications for its economy, politics, and society. This subchapter delves into the multifaceted consequences of Iran's isolation, shedding light on the various dimensions of this issue.

From a diplomatic standpoint, Iran's isolation has strained its relationships with other nations around the world. This has resulted in limited avenues for dialogue and cooperation, making it challenging for Iran to advance its diplomatic interests and address key international concerns. As diplomats, it is crucial to understand the implications of this isolation and explore potential avenues for engagement to bridge the gap between Iran and the global community.

The State of Qatar has emerged as a key player in this scenario, serving as Iran's open window to the world. Despite Iran's isolation, Qatar has maintained robust diplomatic relations with the country, facilitating dialogue and acting as a mediator in regional conflicts. This unique dynamic between Qatar and Iran deserves closer examination, as it has the potential to reshape the geopolitical landscape of the Middle East.

Furthermore, Qatar's economic relations with Iran have played a significant role in mitigating the impact of Iran's isolation. Despite international sanctions, Qatar has continued to engage in trade with Iran, providing a lifeline for the Iranian economy. Additionally, Qatar's investment in various sectors of the Iranian economy has created opportunities for both countries to reap mutual benefits.

Cultural exchange and tourism between Qatar and Iran have also flourished, fostering people-to-people connections and promoting understanding between the two nations. Qatar's commitment to cultural collaboration has allowed Iran to showcase its rich heritage and traditions, contributing to a deeper appreciation of Iranian culture on a global scale.

Energy cooperation between Qatar and Iran has been another crucial aspect of their relationship. Despite being major players in the global energy market, both countries recognize the benefits of collaboration and have explored avenues for joint projects, including shared natural gas fields.

In the realm of politics, Qatar and Iran have formed alliances in regional conflicts, influencing the dynamics of the Middle East. By collaborating on key political issues, both countries have sought to protect their shared interests and maintain stability in the region.

Sports diplomacy, education and academic collaboration, transport and connectivity, security cooperation, and media and information exchange are all areas where Qatar and Iran have found common ground, transcending the barriers of Iran's isolation.

As diplomats, it is imperative to recognize and explore the implications of Iran's isolation and the role that Qatar plays in bridging the gap between Iran and the international community. By understanding the multifaceted dimensions of this issue, diplomats can contribute to fostering dialogue, cooperation, and mutual understanding between Iran and the world.

Qatar's Role as a Bridge to the World

Qatar, a small but influential Gulf nation, has emerged as a key player in bridging the gap between Iran and the rest of the world. In this subchapter, we will explore the various aspects of Qatar's role as a bridge and its impact on diplomacy, trade, culture, energy, politics, sports, education, transport, security, and media exchange between Qatar and Iran.

Diplomatically, Qatar has played a crucial role in facilitating dialogue and negotiations between Iran and other nations. With its neutral stance and diplomatic finesse, Qatar has been able to mediate conflicts, ease tensions, and promote peaceful resolutions. This has been particularly evident in its efforts to mediate the ongoing Gulf crisis, where Qatar has sought to bridge the gap between Iran and its neighboring Gulf countries.

Qatar's economic relations with Iran have also flourished in recent years. Despite international sanctions, Qatar has maintained a robust trade relationship with Iran, becoming a major importer of Iranian goods and a significant investor in the Iranian market. This economic cooperation has not only benefited both nations but has also demonstrated Qatar's commitment to promoting economic integration in the region.

Cultural exchange and tourism have been instrumental in strengthening the ties between Qatar and Iran. Through various cultural events, exhibitions, and festivals, Qatar has showcased Iranian art, music, and traditions, fostering a deeper understanding and appreciation of Iranian culture. Additionally, the increasing number of Iranian tourists visiting Qatar has contributed to the growth of the tourism industry in both countries.

Energy cooperation between Qatar and Iran has been of paramount importance. As two major energy producers, Qatar and Iran have collaborated on joint ventures and energy projects, ensuring a stable supply of energy to the region. This collaboration has not only strengthened their economic ties but has also enhanced energy security in the Gulf.

Politically, Qatar and Iran have found common ground on several regional issues. Both nations share similar viewpoints on regional conflicts and have collaborated on various political initiatives to promote stability and security in the region. Qatar's alliances with Iran have allowed it to exert influence and have a say in regional affairs, enhancing its diplomatic standing.

Sports diplomacy has also played a significant role in bringing Qatar and Iran together. Qatar's hosting of major international sporting events, such as the FIFA World Cup and the Doha Asian Games, has provided a platform for athletes from both countries to compete and engage in cultural exchange, fostering greater understanding and cooperation.

Education and academic collaboration between Qatar and Iran have flourished in recent years. Qatar has welcomed Iranian students to its universities and research institutions, promoting knowledge exchange and fostering intellectual growth. This collaboration has not only benefited the students but has also contributed to the development of both nations' academic sectors.

Transport and connectivity between Qatar and Iran have been a key focus for both nations. Qatar Airways, the national carrier of Qatar, has established direct flights to major Iranian cities, facilitating travel and trade between the two countries. This improved connectivity has opened up new avenues for economic cooperation and cultural exchange.

Qatar and Iran have also collaborated on security matters, particularly in counterterrorism efforts. Sharing a common interest in regional stability, both nations have worked together to combat extremism and ensure the safety and security of the Gulf region.

Lastly, media and information exchange have played a significant role in strengthening Qatar-Iran relations. Qatar-based media outlets, such as Al Jazeera, have provided a platform for diverse perspectives, including those from Iran. This exchange of information and ideas has fostered greater understanding and has contributed to a more nuanced portrayal of Iranian affairs in the region.

In conclusion, Qatar's role as a bridge to the world has been instrumental in fostering diplomatic, economic, cultural, energy, political, sports, educational, transport, security, and media cooperation between Qatar and Iran. Through its strategic initiatives and diplomatic finesse, Qatar has played a pivotal role in bridging the gap and bringing Iran closer to the international community, while also enhancing its own standing on the global stage.

Chapter 2: Qatar-Iran Diplomatic Relations

Historical Overview of Qatar-Iran Diplomatic Relations

Since the establishment of diplomatic relations in 1972, Qatar and Iran have maintained a complex and dynamic relationship. This chapter provides a historical overview of the diplomatic ties between the two nations, highlighting the key milestones that have shaped their relationship.

The early years of Qatar-Iran diplomatic relations were marked by cautious engagement as both countries sought to establish a foundation for cooperation. Despite occasional tensions, the two nations recognized the importance of maintaining diplomatic ties and worked towards fostering mutual understanding.

In the early 1990s, Qatar and Iran found common ground in their shared interest in regional stability and security. This period witnessed significant progress in their diplomatic relations, with both countries engaging in high-level visits and signing various agreements to enhance cooperation in trade, investment, and cultural exchange.

Qatar and Iran have also developed strong economic ties over the years. Iran has become an important trading partner for Qatar, particularly in the energy sector. The two countries have collaborated on several joint ventures and energy projects, contributing to the growth of both their economies.

Cultural exchange and tourism have played a significant role in strengthening Qatar-Iran relations. The two nations have encouraged cultural exchanges, organizing festivals, exhibitions, and artistic performances to promote understanding and appreciation of each other's heritage.

In recent years, Qatar and Iran have deepened their cooperation in the field of education and academia. Numerous student exchange programs and academic collaborations have been established, facilitating knowledge sharing and fostering intellectual growth.

Transport and connectivity have also been areas of focus for Qatar and Iran. The two nations have worked together to improve transportation links, including the establishment of direct flights and the development of infrastructure projects that enhance their connectivity.

Security cooperation has emerged as a crucial aspect of Qatar-Iran relations. Both countries have recognized the importance of joint efforts in combating terrorism and promoting regional stability. They have engaged in intelligence sharing and coordinated security operations, enhancing their mutual security interests.

Media and information exchange have played a significant role in shaping public opinion and perceptions between Qatar and Iran. The two nations have facilitated media partnerships and information sharing, promoting greater understanding and accurate reporting on bilateral issues.

In conclusion, Qatar-Iran diplomatic relations have evolved over the years, encompassing various aspects such as trade, culture, education, and security. Despite occasional challenges, both nations have recognized the mutual benefits of cooperation and have strived to build a strong foundation for their relationship. This chapter provides a comprehensive overview of the historical developments that have shaped Qatar-Iran diplomatic relations, highlighting the progress made and the prospects for future collaboration.

Key Agreements and Treaties between Qatar and Iran

Introduction:

The diplomatic relations between Qatar and Iran have witnessed significant developments over the years, resulting in a range of agreements and treaties that have strengthened ties between the two countries. This subchapter explores the key agreements and treaties that have shaped Qatar-Iran relations across various domains, including trade, culture, energy, politics, security, and more.

Qatar-Iran Diplomatic Relations:

The establishment of diplomatic relations between Qatar and Iran dates back to 1972, with both countries opening embassies in each other's capitals. This initial step laid the foundation for future cooperation and dialogue between the two nations.

Qatar-Iran Trade and Economic Relations:

The signing of a bilateral trade agreement in 1996 paved the way for enhanced economic cooperation between Qatar and Iran. This agreement focused on promoting trade, investment, and joint ventures, thereby bolstering economic ties between the two nations.

Qatar-Iran Cultural Exchange and Tourism:

Cultural exchange and tourism have played a vital role in strengthening people-to-people connections between Qatar and Iran. Several agreements have been signed to promote cultural exchange programs, exhibitions, and festivals, fostering a deeper understanding and appreciation of each other's heritage.

Qatar-Iran Energy Cooperation:

Both Qatar and Iran are major players in the energy sector, and their cooperation in this domain has been crucial. Agreements on the exploration and production of oil and gas, as well as joint ventures in energy-related projects, have solidified the energy cooperation between the two countries.

Qatar-Iran Political Cooperation and Alliances:

Political cooperation between Qatar and Iran has been characterized by regular high-level visits and consultations, demonstrating a shared commitment to regional stability and peace. Several agreements have been signed to foster collaboration on political issues of mutual interest.

Qatar-Iran Sports Diplomacy:

Sports diplomacy has emerged as a significant avenue for fostering goodwill between Qatar and Iran. Agreements on sports exchanges, joint training camps, and organizing friendly matches have created opportunities for athletes and sports enthusiasts from both countries to come together.

Qatar-Iran Education and Academic Collaboration:

The field of education and academia has witnessed growing collaboration between Qatar and Iran. Agreements on student exchanges, joint research programs, and academic conferences have facilitated knowledge-sharing and academic cooperation.

Qatar-Iran Transport and Connectivity:

Enhancing connectivity and transportation links between Qatar and Iran has been a priority. The signing of agreements on air transport, maritime connectivity, and road infrastructure development has facilitated smoother movement of goods and people between the two countries.

Qatar-Iran Security Cooperation:

Given the shared interests and challenges in the region, Qatar and Iran have cooperated closely on security matters. Agreements on intelligence sharing, counterterrorism efforts, and joint military exercises have strengthened the security cooperation between the two nations.

Qatar-Iran Media and Information Exchange:

Recognizing the role of media in shaping public opinion, Qatar and Iran have signed agreements to promote media cooperation and exchange. This collaboration has facilitated the sharing of news, documentaries, and cultural programs, fostering a better understanding of each other's perspectives.

Conclusion:

The numerous agreements and treaties between Qatar and Iran reflect the multifaceted nature of their diplomatic relations. From trade and economics to culture, energy, and security, these agreements have laid the foundation for a comprehensive and mutually beneficial partnership between the two nations. As Qatar continues to bridge the gap and serve as Iran's open window to the world, these agreements will play a vital role in further enhancing cooperation and understanding between the two countries.

Challenges and Controversies in Qatar-Iran Diplomatic Relations

Diplomatic relations between Qatar and Iran have been marked by numerous challenges and controversies over the years. This subchapter explores the multifaceted issues that have impacted the bilateral ties between these two nations, shedding light on the complexities faced by diplomats in navigating this delicate relationship.

One of the primary challenges in Qatar-Iran diplomatic relations is the strained regional dynamics. The ongoing conflicts in the Middle East, particularly in Syria and Yemen, have created a divide between Qatar and

Iran. Qatar's support for various rebel groups in Syria and its involvement in the Saudi-led coalition in Yemen have put it at odds with Iran's regional interests. This has resulted in a divergence of political views and strained the diplomatic ties between the two nations.

Another controversial aspect of Qatar-Iran relations revolves around trade and economic cooperation. Despite the imposition of economic sanctions on Iran, Qatar has maintained a level of economic engagement with its neighbor. This has raised concerns among some nations who view Qatar's trade relations with Iran as a violation of international agreements. The challenge for diplomats lies in striking a balance between maintaining economic ties and adhering to international obligations.

Cultural exchange and tourism between Qatar and Iran have also faced hurdles. Differences in religious and cultural practices, as well as geopolitical tensions, have limited the extent of cultural exchange between the two nations. Qatar's efforts to promote cultural understanding and tourism have been met with skepticism and resistance from certain quarters. Diplomats must navigate these challenges to foster greater people-to-people connections and promote mutual understanding.

Energy cooperation is another area where challenges arise. Qatar, being one of the largest exporters of liquefied natural gas (LNG), competes with Iran in the global energy market. This competition has occasionally strained their energy cooperation and led to disagreements over pricing and market share. Diplomats must work towards finding common ground and mutually beneficial solutions to overcome these challenges.

Political cooperation and alliances have also faced controversies in Qatar-Iran relations. Qatar's independent foreign policy and its support for various political groups in the region have sometimes clashed with Iran's interests. This has resulted in a divergence of political objectives and strained their political cooperation. Diplomats must engage in dialogue and negotiations to bridge these differences and find common ground for collaboration.

In conclusion, Qatar-Iran diplomatic relations face numerous challenges and controversies across various sectors. From regional conflicts to economic cooperation, cultural exchange to energy cooperation, diplomats play a crucial role in navigating these complexities and finding common ground for cooperation. By addressing these challenges head-on, Qatar and Iran can work towards strengthening their bilateral ties and fostering greater understanding and collaboration between their nations.

The Role of Diplomacy in Bridging the Gap

In the complex world of international relations, diplomacy plays a vital role in bridging the gap between nations. This subchapter will delve into the significance of diplomacy in the context of the State of Qatar's relationship with Iran, exploring various dimensions such as trade, culture, energy, politics, sports, education, transport, security, and media.

Diplomacy serves as the cornerstone of Qatar's efforts to engage with Iran, a country that has often been perceived as isolated from the international community. Acting as a bridge, diplomacy facilitates dialogue and understanding, paving the way for cooperation and mutual benefits between nations.

In the realm of trade and economics, diplomacy plays a crucial role in fostering Qatar-Iran relations. Through diplomatic channels, both countries can negotiate trade agreements, resolve disputes, and create an enabling environment for investment and commerce. This diplomatic engagement provides opportunities for economic growth and prosperity, benefiting both Qatar and Iran.

Cultural exchange and tourism are another significant aspect of Qatar-Iran relations, and diplomacy serves as a catalyst in promoting these interactions. Through diplomatic initiatives, cultural programs, and tourism campaigns, Qatar and Iran can enhance people-to-people connections, promoting mutual understanding and appreciation of their respective cultures.

Energy cooperation is another vital area where diplomacy plays a pivotal role. Qatar and Iran, both major energy exporters, can engage in diplomatic negotiations to ensure stable energy markets, explore collaborative projects, and address common challenges in the energy sector. This diplomatic engagement contributes to the overall stability and sustainability of the global energy landscape.

Political cooperation and alliances are strengthened through diplomatic channels. Qatar and Iran can collaborate on regional and global issues, exchanging ideas, perspectives, and expertise. This diplomatic engagement helps in fostering stability, resolving conflicts, and promoting peace in the region.

Sports diplomacy is also an emerging avenue for Qatar and Iran to engage and bridge the gap. Through sports exchanges, joint events, and collaborations, both countries can enhance their people-to-people connections, fostering goodwill and understanding.

Diplomacy also plays a crucial role in promoting education and academic collaboration between Qatar and Iran. Through diplomatic initiatives, both countries can facilitate student exchanges, joint research projects, and academic partnerships, nurturing a knowledge-based society and fostering intellectual growth.

Transport and connectivity are further areas where diplomacy plays a critical role. By engaging in diplomatic dialogues, Qatar and Iran can enhance transportation links, explore infrastructure projects, and improve connectivity, facilitating the movement of goods, people, and ideas between the two countries.

Security cooperation is of paramount importance in the region, and diplomacy serves as a means to address common security challenges and foster stability. Through diplomatic channels, Qatar and Iran can collaborate on counter-terrorism efforts, intelligence sharing, and defense cooperation, working towards a secure and stable region.

Lastly, media and information exchange are vital in enhancing bilateral relations. Diplomatic engagement allows for the exchange of journalists, media professionals, and information, promoting accurate and unbiased reporting, and fostering a better understanding of each other's perspectives.

In conclusion, diplomacy plays a pivotal role in bridging the gap between the State of Qatar and Iran. Through diplomatic initiatives, both countries can strengthen their trade, cultural, energy, political, sports, education, transport, security, and media relations. By engaging in dialogue, diplomacy allows Qatar and Iran to build trust, understanding, and cooperation, creating a foundation for a mutually beneficial and sustainable partnership.

Chapter 3: Qatar-Iran Trade and Economic Relations

The Importance of Trade between Qatar and Iran

In recent years, the trade relationship between Qatar and Iran has emerged as a vital component in the diplomatic and economic landscape of both nations. This subchapter aims to underscore the significance of this trade partnership and shed light on its multifaceted benefits for both countries.

Qatar-Iran Trade and Economic Relations

Trade between Qatar and Iran has experienced remarkable growth, bolstering economic ties and enhancing bilateral cooperation. Both nations recognize the potential for expanding their economies through mutually beneficial trade arrangements. Iran, with its vast natural resources and diverse manufacturing sector, offers Qatar a reliable source of goods and commodities, while Qatar provides Iran with access to its lucrative markets and investment opportunities. This symbiotic relationship has resulted in increased trade volumes, contributing to the economic growth of both nations.

Qatar-Iran Energy Cooperation

Energy cooperation stands as a cornerstone of the relationship between Qatar and Iran. With Qatar's status as the world's largest exporter of liquefied natural gas (LNG) and Iran's substantial reserves of oil and gas, the two countries have found common ground in energy collaboration. This partnership ensures stability in the global energy market and serves as a catalyst for economic development in the region.

Qatar-Iran Cultural Exchange and Tourism

Cultural exchange and tourism play a pivotal role in fostering understanding and friendship between nations. Qatar and Iran have actively engaged in promoting cultural dialogue, facilitating the exchange of ideas, arts, and heritage. This cultural synergy has not only strengthened the bonds between the people of both nations but also boosted tourism, attracting visitors from around the world to explore the rich cultural heritage and natural beauty of both countries.

Qatar-Iran Political Cooperation and Alliances

Political cooperation and alliances between Qatar and Iran have been instrumental in maintaining stability in the region. Both nations have played a significant role in mediating conflicts and promoting peaceful resolutions. Their shared interests and diplomatic ties have allowed them to effectively address regional challenges, contributing to a more secure and prosperous Middle East.

Qatar-Iran Education and Academic Collaboration

Education and academic collaboration between Qatar and Iran have flourished in recent years. Both countries have established partnerships in the field of higher education, facilitating student exchanges and joint research projects. This collaboration not only benefits the individuals involved but also promotes knowledge sharing and the development of a skilled workforce, which is crucial for the progress of both nations.

In conclusion, the importance of trade between Qatar and Iran cannot be overstated. Through economic, cultural, political, and educational collaboration, both countries have fostered a mutually beneficial relationship that has contributed to their respective growth and development. This trade partnership serves as a bridge, connecting Qatar and Iran and opening up new avenues for cooperation in various domains. As diplomats, it is essential to recognize and appreciate the significance of this trade relationship and strive to further strengthen and diversify it for the betterment of both nations and the region as a whole.

Key Industries and Sectors in Qatar-Iran Trade

The trade relationship between Qatar and Iran has witnessed significant growth over the years, with both countries recognizing the immense potential for economic cooperation. This subchapter explores the key industries and sectors that have played a vital role in facilitating trade between Qatar and Iran.

One of the primary industries that have flourished in the Qatar-Iran trade is the energy sector. Qatar, being the largest exporter of liquefied natural gas (LNG) in the world, has found a reliable market in Iran, which has a growing demand for energy resources. The energy cooperation between the two countries has not only strengthened their economic ties but also fostered a sense of mutual trust and collaboration.

Another significant sector in Qatar-Iran trade is construction and infrastructure development. Qatar's ambitious projects, such as the FIFA World Cup 2022 and the Qatar National Vision 2030, have opened up immense opportunities for Iranian companies to contribute their expertise in various construction projects. Iranian firms have been actively involved in the construction of stadiums, hotels, and transportation infrastructure, further enhancing trade relations between the two nations.

The tourism sector has also witnessed a surge in Qatar-Iran trade. Qatar's efforts to diversify its economy and promote tourism have attracted a growing number of Iranian tourists. Qatar's world-class hotels, cultural attractions, and vibrant shopping destinations have become a popular choice for Iranian visitors, contributing to the growth of the tourism sector and fostering cultural exchange between the two countries.

The education and academic collaboration sector has also played a crucial role in strengthening Qatar-Iran trade relations. Qatar's prestigious universities and research institutions have attracted Iranian students and scholars, leading to knowledge exchange and academic partnerships. This has not only enhanced the educational landscape in both countries but also deepened cultural understanding and people-to-people connections.

Additionally, transport and connectivity have been instrumental in facilitating trade between Qatar and Iran. Qatar Airways, the national carrier of Qatar, has established direct flights to major Iranian cities, providing convenient travel options for business and leisure travelers. This has significantly contributed to the growth of trade and tourism between the two nations.

In conclusion, the key industries and sectors in Qatar-Iran trade encompass energy, construction, tourism, education, and transport. These sectors have not only promoted economic cooperation but also fostered cultural exchange, academic collaboration, and people-to-people connections. As Qatar and Iran continue to strengthen their diplomatic, economic, and cultural ties, these industries will play a vital role in bridging the gap and opening up new avenues for cooperation and development.

Challenges and Opportunities in Qatar-Iran Economic Relations

Introduction:

The economic relations between Qatar and Iran have witnessed both challenges and opportunities in recent years. As two significant players in the Middle East, these countries have been actively exploring avenues to strengthen their ties and promote mutual benefits. This subchapter aims to discuss the challenges that have hindered Qatar-Iran economic relations, as well as the opportunities that exist for further collaboration in various sectors.

Challenges:

1. Sanctions and International Pressure: The reimposition of sanctions on Iran by the international community has posed challenges for Qatar's economic engagement with Iran. This has limited the ability of Qatari businesses to invest and trade with their Iranian counterparts.

2. Geopolitical Tensions: The ongoing geopolitical tensions in the region have had an impact on Qatar-Iran economic relations. The conflicting interests of other regional powers have made it difficult for Qatar and Iran to fully realize the potential of their economic partnership.

Opportunities:

1. Trade and Investment: Qatar and Iran have the potential to significantly enhance their bilateral trade and investment cooperation. Qatar's expertise in finance and infrastructure development, coupled with Iran's vast consumer market and natural resources, creates opportunities for mutually beneficial economic partnerships.

2. Energy Cooperation: Both Qatar and Iran are major players in the energy sector. Strengthening energy cooperation between the two countries could lead to joint ventures in oil and gas exploration, production, and distribution, benefiting both nations.

3. Tourism and Cultural Exchange: Qatar and Iran can further promote tourism and cultural exchange between their countries. Qatar's booming tourism industry and Iran's rich cultural heritage make them attractive destinations for travelers. Encouraging more people-to-people interactions can foster understanding and create additional economic opportunities.

4. Academic Collaboration: Qatar and Iran can explore opportunities for academic collaboration, including student exchange programs and joint research initiatives. Sharing knowledge and expertise in various fields can contribute to the development of both countries.

Conclusion:

Despite the challenges faced, Qatar and Iran can overcome these obstacles by focusing on the numerous opportunities for economic cooperation. By leveraging their respective strengths and capitalizing on sectors such as trade, energy, tourism, and education, Qatar and Iran can foster a more robust economic partnership. This will not only benefit the two countries but also contribute to regional stability and prosperity. Diplomats can play a crucial role in facilitating dialogue and finding common ground to enhance Qatar-Iran economic relations and build a more interconnected and prosperous Middle East.

The Potential for Economic Growth and Cooperation

In recent years, the State of Qatar has emerged as a key player in the Middle East, with its strategic location and robust economy. This subchapter explores the potential for economic growth and cooperation between Qatar and Iran, highlighting the various sectors that are ripe for collaboration.

Qatar-Iran Diplomatic Relations:

Diplomatic relations between Qatar and Iran have witnessed a significant upturn in recent years. Both countries have recognized the importance of dialogue and cooperation in maintaining regional stability and addressing common challenges. Strengthening diplomatic ties between the two nations opens doors for enhanced economic cooperation.

Qatar-Iran Trade and Economic Relations:

Qatar and Iran have a long history of trade ties, with their geographical proximity offering immense potential for increased economic collaboration. Both countries can leverage their respective strengths to bolster bilateral trade and investment. Qatar, with its financial resources, can provide investment opportunities in various sectors in Iran, while Iran, with its vast natural resources, can offer Qatar access to a diversified market.

Qatar-Iran Cultural Exchange and Tourism:

Cultural exchange and tourism play a crucial role in fostering people-to-people connections and promoting understanding between nations. Qatar and Iran can explore opportunities for cultural exchange programs, encouraging tourism and promoting each other's rich cultural heritage. This can lead to increased economic activity in the travel and tourism sectors, benefiting both countries.

Qatar-Iran Energy Cooperation:

Both Qatar and Iran are major players in the energy sector, with significant reserves of oil and gas. Cooperation in the energy sector can lead to mutual benefits, such as joint ventures in exploring, producing, and exporting energy resources. Qatar's expertise in liquefied natural gas (LNG) and Iran's vast reserves can create a win-win situation for both countries.

Qatar-Iran Political Cooperation and Alliances:

Political cooperation between Qatar and Iran can have far-reaching implications for regional stability. By aligning their interests and working together, the two nations can address common challenges, such as terrorism and regional conflicts. This cooperation can also foster economic growth by creating a stable environment for trade and investment.

Qatar-Iran Sports Diplomacy:

Sports diplomacy has proven to be an effective tool in bridging cultural gaps and fostering goodwill between nations. Qatar and Iran can explore opportunities for sports collaborations, such as hosting joint sporting events and exchanging expertise in sports management. This can not only enhance people-to-people connections but also boost tourism and stimulate economic growth in the sports industry.

Qatar-Iran Education and Academic Collaboration:

Collaboration in the education sector can strengthen ties between Qatar and Iran. Academic exchanges, joint research projects, and scholarships can facilitate knowledge transfer and skill development, benefiting both countries. This collaboration can also pave the way for increased educational opportunities for students from both nations.

Qatar-Iran Transport and Connectivity:

Improving transport and connectivity between Qatar and Iran can unlock new economic opportunities. Enhancing air, sea, and land connectivity can facilitate trade, tourism, and people-to-people exchanges. Investments in infrastructure projects, such as ports, airports, and highways, can contribute to economic growth and regional integration.

Qatar-Iran Security Cooperation:

Enhancing security cooperation between Qatar and Iran is essential for maintaining regional stability and countering common security threats. Collaborative efforts in sharing intelligence, conducting joint military exercises, and addressing issues such as terrorism and cyber threats can create a secure environment for economic growth and cooperation.

Qatar-Iran Media and Information Exchange:

Promoting media and information exchange between Qatar and Iran can foster better understanding and facilitate business partnerships. Facilitating the exchange of news, cultural programs, and documentaries can bridge the gap between the two nations and create a positive environment for economic cooperation.

In conclusion, the State of Qatar and Iran have significant potential for economic growth and cooperation across various sectors. By leveraging their complementary strengths and fostering diplomatic ties, both nations can create a conducive environment for trade, tourism, cultural exchange, and investment. This collaboration can not only benefit Qatar and Iran but also contribute to regional stability and prosperity. Diplomats have a crucial role to play in facilitating and expanding these opportunities, strengthening the ties between the State of Qatar and Iran.

Chapter 4: Qatar-Iran Cultural Exchange and Tourism

Cultural Similarities and Differences between Qatar and Iran

In the subchapter "Cultural Similarities and Differences between Qatar and Iran," we explore the unique aspects that both countries bring to the table, as well as the shared cultural values that have influenced their historical relations. Understanding these cultural nuances is crucial for diplomats engaging in Qatar-Iran diplomatic, trade, economic, and cultural exchanges, as it forms the foundation for building strong and meaningful connections.

Qatar and Iran, despite their geographical proximity, possess distinct cultural identities that have been shaped by their respective histories, traditions, and religious practices. Qatar, an Arab nation, is deeply rooted in Islamic traditions and has embraced a modern and cosmopolitan lifestyle. On the other hand, Iran is a country with a rich Persian heritage, known for its vibrant art, literature, and ancient civilization.

One of the striking similarities between Qatar and Iran is their shared Islamic faith. Both nations are predominantly Muslim, and Islam plays a significant role in shaping their societies and cultural practices. This shared religious foundation has facilitated the development of strong cultural ties between the two countries, fostering mutual understanding and respect.

Moreover, Qatar and Iran have a deep appreciation for art and literature. Qatar, with its world-class museums and cultural initiatives, has become a hub for art and creativity in the Middle East. Similarly, Iran boasts a rich artistic heritage, with Persian literature and poetry dating back centuries. This cultural affinity has led to fruitful collaborations in the fields of art, literature, and cultural exchange, promoting a deeper understanding of each other's traditions and fostering cultural diplomacy.

Despite these cultural similarities, Qatar and Iran also have their fair share of differences. The Qatari society, influenced by its vast expatriate population, has adopted a more liberal and progressive approach to social issues. In contrast, Iran has a more conservative outlook, with a strong emphasis on religious and traditional values. Understanding and respecting these cultural differences is crucial for effective diplomatic engagement between the two nations.

As diplomats navigate the complexities of Qatar-Iran relations, it is essential to recognize the cultural similarities and differences between these two nations. By fostering cultural exchange, promoting tourism, and encouraging people-to-people interactions, diplomats can build bridges, strengthen mutual understanding, and create a solid foundation for collaboration in various sectors such as trade, education, energy, and security.

In conclusion, Qatar and Iran share a common Islamic heritage, but their distinct cultural identities and values shape their societies differently. Recognizing and appreciating these cultural similarities and differences is vital for diplomats engaging in Qatar-Iran relations, as it forms the basis for fruitful collaborations and strengthens mutual understanding and respect.

Promoting Cultural Exchange and Understanding

In the fast-paced and interconnected world we live in today, fostering cultural exchange and understanding has become paramount for nations seeking to build stronger diplomatic relationships. The State of Qatar, often referred to as Iran's open window to the world, recognizes the significance of promoting cultural exchange as a means to bridge the gap between nations and create a pathway for deeper understanding and collaboration.

The cultural exchange between Qatar and Iran has played a crucial role in shaping the diplomatic relations between the two countries. Through various initiatives and programs, both nations have strived to facilitate the exchange of cultural traditions, heritage, and values. This exchange has been recognized as a powerful tool to break down barriers and overcome misconceptions that may exist between Qatar and Iran.

Qatar has taken significant steps to solidify its commitment to cultural exchange and understanding. The nation has actively encouraged tourism and cultural visits between the two countries, allowing citizens and tourists alike to experience the rich history, art, and architecture of both Qatar and Iran. These initiatives have not only strengthened the bonds between the people of both nations but have also provided economic opportunities through increased tourism and cultural industries.

Furthermore, Qatar and Iran have collaborated extensively in the field of education and academic collaboration. Through student exchanges, joint research projects, and academic partnerships, both countries have facilitated the transfer of knowledge and expertise. This collaboration has not only enriched the academic landscape in both nations but has also fostered a broader understanding of each other's culture, traditions, and values.

The promotion of cultural exchange and understanding has also extended to the sports arena. Qatar and Iran have embraced sports diplomacy, using sporting events as a platform to bring people together, foster goodwill, and build lasting connections. Through joint sporting initiatives, such as friendly matches and tournaments, both nations have showcased the power of sports in transcending boundaries and promoting unity.

In conclusion, the State of Qatar recognizes the immense value of promoting cultural exchange and understanding as a means to bridge the gap between nations. Through initiatives focused on tourism, education, sports diplomacy, and more, Qatar has actively worked to build stronger diplomatic, economic, and cultural ties with Iran. By embracing such initiatives, Qatar continues to serve as Iran's open window to the world, providing a platform for increased dialogue, collaboration, and mutual understanding between the two nations.

The Role of Tourism in Strengthening Qatar-Iran Relations

As the State of Qatar seeks to bridge the gap between Iran and the rest of the world, tourism plays a vital role in bolstering the diplomatic, economic, cultural, and social ties between these two nations. This subchapter will delve into the significance of tourism in strengthening Qatar-Iran relations, highlighting its impact on various aspects of bilateral cooperation.

Qatar-Iran Diplomatic Relations:

Tourism acts as a catalyst in enhancing diplomatic ties between Qatar and Iran. By promoting people-to-people interactions, tourism fosters understanding and trust, ultimately leading to stronger diplomatic relations. The exchange of high-level visits and cultural delegations facilitated by tourism initiatives creates opportunities for dialogue and cooperation.

Qatar-Iran Trade and Economic Relations:

Tourism acts as a gateway for increased trade and economic cooperation between Qatar and Iran. As tourists from both countries explore each other's markets, they enhance bilateral trade opportunities. Investments in the tourism sector also contribute to economic growth, generating employment and boosting local businesses in both nations.

Qatar-Iran Cultural Exchange and Tourism:

Tourism serves as a powerful tool for cultural exchange, allowing Qatar and Iran to showcase their rich heritage, traditions, and artistic expressions. Cultural tourism fosters mutual understanding, appreciation, and respect for each other's diversity, thereby strengthening the cultural ties between the two nations.

Qatar-Iran Energy Cooperation:

Tourism can play a significant role in promoting energy cooperation between Qatar and Iran. As tourists visit energy-related sites and gain insights into each other's energy sectors, they facilitate knowledge sharing and potential collaboration in the field of energy production, exploration, and technology.

Qatar-Iran Political Cooperation and Alliances:

Tourism can contribute to political cooperation and alliances between Qatar and Iran. As visitors from both nations engage in political discussions and participate in conferences, symposiums, and seminars, they lay the groundwork for deeper political cooperation, leading to potential alliances on regional and international issues.

Qatar-Iran Sports Diplomacy:

Tourism, particularly in sports, enhances Qatar-Iran relations. Sporting events, such as friendly matches, tournaments, and joint training programs, provide a platform for athletes, coaches, and sports enthusiasts from both nations to come together, fostering friendship, cooperation, and goodwill.

Qatar-Iran Education and Academic Collaboration:

Tourism facilitates educational and academic collaboration between Qatar and Iran. Students, researchers, and academics benefit from exchange programs, joint research initiatives, and educational partnerships, promoting knowledge transfer, innovation, and intellectual growth.

Qatar-Iran Transport and Connectivity:

Tourism contributes to improved transport and connectivity between Qatar and Iran. Enhanced air, sea, and land connectivity through tourism-related infrastructure investments and increased flights create convenient travel options for tourists, bolstering trade, tourism, and people-to-people exchanges.

Qatar-Iran Security Cooperation:

Tourism can also play a role in strengthening security cooperation between Qatar and Iran. Through tourism-related security initiatives, including information sharing, joint training, and intelligence cooperation, the two nations can collaborate in addressing common security challenges and ensuring the safety of tourists.

Qatar-Iran Media and Information Exchange:

Tourism facilitates media and information exchange between Qatar and Iran. As journalists, bloggers, and content creators explore each other's countries, they promote accurate information dissemination, enabling a better understanding of the cultures, societies, and developments in both nations.

In conclusion, tourism serves as a powerful tool in strengthening Qatar-Iran relations across various sectors. By facilitating diplomatic, economic, cultural, and social interactions, tourism paves the way for enhanced cooperation and mutual understanding between these two nations, creating a solid foundation for a strong and enduring partnership.

Challenges and Future Prospects for Cultural Exchange

In today's interconnected world, cultural exchange plays a pivotal role in fostering understanding and cooperation between nations. The State of Qatar and Iran have a long history of cultural exchange, which has not only strengthened their bilateral relations but also opened new avenues for dialogue and cooperation. However, there are several challenges that need to be addressed for the successful continuation of this exchange, and there are also promising prospects for further growth.

One of the main challenges for cultural exchange between Qatar and Iran is the prevailing geopolitical tensions in the region. These tensions have often led to strained diplomatic relations and hindered the smooth flow of people and ideas between the two countries. Overcoming these challenges requires a concerted effort from both sides to prioritize cultural exchange as a means of bridging the gap and promoting mutual understanding.

Another challenge is the language barrier. While Arabic is the official language in Qatar and Persian is the official language in Iran, both countries have made significant efforts to promote the teaching and learning of each other's languages. However, there is still a need for further investment in language education and cultural programs to facilitate effective communication and cultural understanding.

Despite these challenges, there are promising prospects for the future of cultural exchange between Qatar and Iran. The State of Qatar has been actively promoting its cultural heritage and identity through initiatives such as the Qatar Museums Authority and the Doha Film Institute. These efforts have not only attracted international attention but have also created opportunities for collaboration and cultural exchange with Iran.

Furthermore, the growing tourism industry in both countries presents a unique opportunity for cultural exchange. Qatar's commitment to becoming a global tourism hub and Iran's rich cultural heritage and historical sites make them attractive destinations for travelers. By promoting tourism and facilitating cultural interactions, both countries can further enhance their cultural ties and promote a positive image internationally.

In conclusion, while there are challenges that need to be addressed, the future prospects for cultural exchange between Qatar and Iran are promising. By prioritizing cultural exchange, investing in language education, and leveraging the growing tourism industry, both countries can strengthen their bilateral relations and promote greater understanding and cooperation. Cultural exchange has the power to bridge the gap and serve as a catalyst for positive change, not only between Qatar and Iran but also within the broader context of international diplomacy and cooperation.

Chapter 5: Qatar-Iran Energy Cooperation

Qatar and Iran's Energy Resources and Production

As two prominent players in the global energy market, Qatar and Iran possess vast energy resources and have been actively involved in the production and distribution of oil and gas. This subchapter aims to shed light on the energy cooperation between these countries and its implications for various domains such as trade, economy, politics, and security.

Qatar, renowned for its liquefied natural gas (LNG) reserves, has emerged as a leading LNG exporter globally. Its advanced technology and substantial investments have allowed it to tap into its vast offshore gas fields, making it a key supplier of clean energy to countries worldwide. On the other hand, Iran, with its abundant oil and gas reserves, has been a significant player in the global energy market for decades.

The energy cooperation between Qatar and Iran has been mutually beneficial, fostering trade and economic relations. Qatar's LNG exports have played a crucial role in meeting Iran's growing energy demands, particularly in the face of international sanctions. This cooperation has not only helped Iran maintain its energy security but has also provided an opportunity for Qatar to expand its market reach.

Moreover, Qatar and Iran's energy ties have extended beyond trade, contributing to political cooperation and alliances. The two countries have collaborated on various regional energy projects, such as the development of gas pipelines and joint ventures, fostering closer ties and enhancing their influence in the region. This cooperation has also facilitated diplomatic relations, as shared interests in energy security have provided a platform for dialogue and negotiation.

In addition to economic and political cooperation, Qatar and Iran's energy collaboration has paved the way for cultural exchange and tourism. As Qatar's economy diversifies, the country has increasingly focused on promoting its cultural heritage and attracting tourists. Iran, with its rich history and cultural treasures, has become an attractive destination for Qatari tourists, fostering people-to-people exchanges and enhancing cultural understanding between the two nations.

Furthermore, the energy cooperation has facilitated transport and connectivity between Qatar and Iran. Collaborative efforts in developing transportation infrastructure, such as ports and pipelines, have improved connectivity and facilitated the movement of goods and people, strengthening trade and economic ties.

Lastly, the two countries have also cooperated in the fields of education, academia, and sports diplomacy. Academic collaborations and student exchanges have promoted knowledge sharing and cultural understanding. Additionally, Qatar and Iran's joint efforts in sports diplomacy have not only fostered friendly competition but have also presented opportunities for cultural exchange and dialogue.

In conclusion, Qatar and Iran's energy resources and production have played a vital role in shaping their diplomatic relations across various sectors. From trade and economy to politics and culture, the energy cooperation between these nations has created opportunities for collaboration and dialogue, strengthening their ties and promoting regional stability.

The Significance of Energy Cooperation between Qatar and Iran

Energy cooperation between Qatar and Iran holds immense significance not only for the two countries but also for the entire region. This subchapter aims to highlight the key aspects of this cooperation and shed light on its implications for various sectors, including trade, economy, politics, security, and more.

The State of Qatar and Iran share a strong bond in terms of energy cooperation. Both countries possess vast reserves of natural gas, making them prominent players in the global energy market. Qatar, being the world's largest exporter of liquefied natural gas (LNG), and Iran, possessing the second-largest gas reserves globally, have recognized the benefits of collaboration in this sector.

Qatar-Iran energy cooperation has contributed significantly to the economic ties between the two nations. The exchange of expertise and technology has enhanced the extraction and production capabilities of both countries, leading to increased revenue generation. Furthermore, joint ventures and investments in the energy sector have opened new avenues for trade and economic growth.

Diplomatically, Qatar and Iran have leveraged their energy cooperation to strengthen their relations. The energy sector serves as a catalyst for diplomatic engagements, facilitating dialogue and building trust between the two nations. Regular high-level meetings and consultations on energy-related matters have created a platform for broader discussions on various regional and global issues.

Moreover, the energy partnership between Qatar and Iran has wider implications for regional security and stability. By fostering collaboration in this sector, the two countries have developed mutual interests that promote peace and cooperation in the region. This shared vision of stability has led to joint efforts in addressing common challenges and conflicts, thereby contributing to the overall security of the region.

Furthermore, energy cooperation between Qatar and Iran has paved the way for cultural exchange and tourism. The increased connectivity between the two countries has facilitated people-to-people interactions, promoting cultural understanding and tourism opportunities. This exchange has not only enriched the cultural fabric of both nations but has also attracted tourists from around the world, boosting the tourism industry.

In conclusion, the significance of energy cooperation between Qatar and Iran cannot be overstated. It serves as a foundation for robust diplomatic, trade, economic, and cultural relations. This collaboration has contributed to the growth and development of both countries while fostering regional security and stability. As Qatar acts as Iran's open window to the world, energy cooperation remains a crucial aspect of their multifaceted partnership.

Joint Ventures and Projects in the Energy Sector

The energy sector plays a crucial role in the economic development and growth of nations. It serves as the backbone of industrialization and a catalyst for progress. In the book "State of Qatar: Bridging the Gap - Iran's Open Window to the World," we explore the joint ventures and projects in the energy sector between Qatar and Iran, showcasing their significance in strengthening diplomatic, trade, economic, and cultural ties.

Qatar and Iran, despite their geographical proximity, have historically faced challenges in their diplomatic relations. However, in recent years, Qatar has emerged as a bridge, connecting Iran with the rest of the world. One of the key areas where this connection is evident is in the energy sector. Both countries boast vast reserves of natural resources, including oil and gas, making them natural partners in the field.

Qatar and Iran's energy cooperation goes beyond mere resource extraction. They have joined forces in various joint ventures and projects aimed at maximizing their potential and ensuring long-term sustainability. These projects encompass exploration, production, refining, and distribution of energy resources. By pooling their resources and expertise, Qatar and Iran have created a synergy that benefits both nations and the wider international community.

One of the notable joint ventures in the energy sector is the development of the South Pars/North Field, the world's largest gas field, shared by Qatar and Iran. This collaboration has resulted in increased production and enhanced energy security for both countries. Additionally, joint ventures in petrochemical plants and LNG facilities have further solidified their energy cooperation.

The collaboration in the energy sector has not only been limited to commercial projects but also encompasses research and development initiatives. Qatar and Iran have established academic collaborations to promote knowledge exchange and innovation in the energy field. This partnership ensures a continuous flow of skilled professionals and experts, contributing to the sustainable growth of both nations.

Moreover, the joint ventures and projects in the energy sector have had a positive impact on other areas of cooperation between Qatar and Iran. They have paved the way for increased trade and economic relations, cultural exchange, tourism, political alliances, sports diplomacy, education, transport, connectivity, security cooperation, and media information exchange.

In conclusion, the joint ventures and projects in the energy sector between Qatar and Iran have played a vital role in bridging the gap between these nations. They have not only strengthened diplomatic relations but have also fostered cooperation in various other fields. The energy sector serves as a foundation for sustainable growth and prosperity, underscoring the importance of continued collaboration between Qatar and Iran.

The Role of Energy Cooperation in Regional Stability

In the ever-changing geopolitical landscape, energy cooperation plays a crucial role in maintaining regional stability. This subchapter explores the significance of energy cooperation between the State of Qatar and Iran, and how it contributes to a more stable and interconnected region.

Energy cooperation between Qatar and Iran has long been recognized as a cornerstone of their diplomatic relations. The two countries share vast reserves of natural gas, and their collaboration in the energy sector has not only strengthened their bilateral ties but also contributed to regional stability. By working together, Qatar and Iran have been able to ensure a steady supply of energy to meet the growing demands of the region, thereby reducing the risk of energy shortages and potential conflicts.

The State of Qatar, often seen as Iran's open window to the world, has been instrumental in bridging the gap between Iran and the international community. Through energy cooperation, Qatar has facilitated Iran's integration into the global energy market, allowing it to export its vast energy resources and thereby improving its economic prospects. This has not only benefited Iran but also contributed to regional stability by providing economic incentives for peaceful cooperation.

Furthermore, energy cooperation between Qatar and Iran has extended beyond economic benefits. It has also fostered cultural exchange and tourism between the two nations. As people from different backgrounds interact and engage in business and cultural exchanges, mutual understanding and appreciation are enhanced. This cultural exchange promotes tolerance and harmony, contributing to a more stable region.

Moreover, energy cooperation has provided a platform for political cooperation and alliances between Qatar and Iran. Through joint energy projects and collaborations, the two countries have been able to strengthen their political ties and build trust. This has facilitated dialogue and cooperation on regional issues, fostering stability and security in the region.

In conclusion, energy cooperation between the State of Qatar and Iran plays a pivotal role in regional stability. By ensuring a steady supply of energy, promoting economic growth, fostering cultural exchange, and strengthening political alliances, energy cooperation contributes to a more interconnected and stable region. It is through such collaborations that the State of Qatar continues to serve as Iran's open window to the world, bridging the gap and promoting peace and prosperity for all.

Chapter 6: Qatar-Iran Political Cooperation and Alliances

Qatar and Iran's Shared Political Interests

In the intricate web of international relations, the State of Qatar and Iran have found themselves closely connected through shared political interests. Despite their geographical distance, these two nations have forged a unique alliance that has opened new horizons for diplomacy, trade, cultural exchange, and much more. This subchapter explores the multifaceted dimensions of Qatar and Iran's political cooperation and alliances, shedding light on the vital role they play in shaping regional dynamics.

Diplomats in search of a deeper understanding of the relationship between Qatar and Iran will find a compelling narrative that challenges preconceived notions. Often portrayed as adversaries, the State of Qatar and Iran have managed to build a robust diplomatic bond, characterized by mutual respect and shared strategic objectives. This chapter delves into the factors that have facilitated this alliance, including a common stance on regional security, a commitment to stability, and a desire for economic prosperity.

Qatar-Iran Diplomatic Relations have flourished over the years, with both countries engaging in regular high-level exchanges. This subchapter examines the diplomatic initiatives taken by Qatar and Iran to foster dialogue and cooperation, showcasing the significance of these efforts in maintaining peace and stability in the region.

The trade and economic relations between Qatar and Iran have proven to be mutually beneficial, as both nations recognize the potential for growth and development. By exploring the various sectors in which these two countries collaborate, including energy, tourism, and transportation, this section offers diplomats valuable insights into the economic opportunities that arise from Qatar and Iran's cooperation.

Furthermore, the cultural exchange and tourism between Qatar and Iran have strengthened the bonds between their people, fostering a deeper understanding and appreciation of each other's rich heritage. This subchapter highlights the initiatives taken to promote cultural exchanges and enhance tourism, showcasing how these efforts contribute to building bridges between the two nations.

Additionally, Qatar and Iran's energy cooperation has played a pivotal role in ensuring a stable energy market and meeting the demands of the global economy. This section explores the dynamics of their energy partnership, delving into the joint ventures and projects that have solidified their collaboration.

Qatar and Iran's shared political interests extend beyond bilateral relations, as they have also formed alliances on various regional issues. This subchapter analyzes the strategic alignments between the two countries and their joint efforts to address common challenges, such as regional conflicts and security concerns.

In conclusion, this subchapter provides diplomats with a comprehensive understanding of the shared political interests between Qatar and Iran. By examining their diplomatic relations, trade and economic cooperation, cultural exchange and tourism, energy partnership, political alliances, and more, it becomes clear that Qatar and Iran have successfully bridged the gap, creating an open window to the world for both nations. The State of Qatar and Iran's unique alliance serves as a model for diplomatic engagement and showcases the power of collaboration in shaping regional dynamics.

Key Alliances and Cooperation between Qatar and Iran

Diplomats and individuals interested in Qatar's relationship with Iran will find this subchapter, titled "Key Alliances and Cooperation between Qatar and Iran," informative and enlightening. This subchapter delves into the various facets of diplomatic, economic, cultural, and political cooperation between the State of Qatar and Iran, shedding light on the symbiotic nature of their relationship.

Qatar-Iran Diplomatic Relations:

The diplomatic relations between Qatar and Iran have been marked by mutual respect and understanding. Both countries have maintained embassies in each other's capitals, facilitating regular high-level exchanges and fostering open lines of communication to address regional and international issues.

Qatar-Iran Trade and Economic Relations:

The economic ties between Qatar and Iran have witnessed significant growth in recent years. Trade agreements and investments have flourished, paving the way for enhanced bilateral cooperation. Both countries have recognized the potential to exploit their geographical proximity and utilize their respective resources, leading to mutually beneficial economic partnerships.

Qatar-Iran Cultural Exchange and Tourism:

Cultural exchange and tourism play a vital role in strengthening the bond between Qatar and Iran. The exchange of artistic, literary, and intellectual ideas has fostered a deeper understanding of each other's rich cultural heritage. Furthermore, the promotion of tourism between the two countries has allowed citizens to explore the diverse landscapes, historical sites, and vibrant traditions.

Qatar-Iran Energy Cooperation:

Energy cooperation between Qatar and Iran has been instrumental in meeting the energy demands of both nations and the global market. Qatar's expertise in liquefied natural gas (LNG) production and Iran's vast reserves of natural gas have led to collaborative efforts in the energy sector, ensuring a stable and reliable supply of energy for the region and beyond.

Qatar-Iran Political Cooperation and Alliances:

Qatar and Iran share common interests and concerns in regional politics, leading to strategic alliances on various fronts. Both countries have worked together to address regional conflicts, promote stability, and facilitate dialogue between conflicting parties. Their collective efforts have contributed to peace-building initiatives and conflict resolution in the region.

Qatar-Iran Sports Diplomacy:

Sports diplomacy has emerged as an effective tool for enhancing bilateral relations between Qatar and Iran. Friendly sports competitions, joint training camps, and the exchange of athletes have fostered a spirit of camaraderie and friendship, transcending political boundaries and promoting people-to-people connections.

Qatar-Iran Education and Academic Collaboration:

Collaboration in the field of education and academia has allowed Qatar and Iran to share knowledge, research, and expertise. Joint academic programs, faculty exchanges, and research collaborations have strengthened intellectual ties, fostering innovation and promoting cultural understanding.

Qatar-Iran Transport and Connectivity:

Enhanced transport and connectivity between Qatar and Iran have facilitated the movement of goods and people, further strengthening their economic ties. Air and maritime connectivity, as well as the development of transport infrastructure, have played a crucial role in bolstering trade and tourism between the two countries.

Qatar-Iran Security Cooperation:

Security cooperation between Qatar and Iran has been vital in addressing common security challenges and maintaining regional stability. Intelligence sharing, joint military exercises, and cooperation in counterterrorism efforts have been instrumental in combating threats and ensuring the safety of both nations.

Qatar-Iran Media and Information Exchange:

Media and information exchange between Qatar and Iran have facilitated a better understanding of each other's perspectives, contributing to a more balanced and nuanced narrative. Collaborative journalism projects, cultural exchanges, and the sharing of media resources have promoted accurate reporting and cultural appreciation.

In conclusion, this subchapter highlights the key alliances and cooperation between Qatar and Iran, shedding light on the multifaceted relationship between the two countries. From diplomatic and economic ties to cultural exchange and security cooperation, the State of Qatar and Iran have found common ground and forged a path towards a stronger and more prosperous future.

Challenges and Controversies in Qatar-Iran Political Cooperation

In the realm of politics, Qatar and Iran have had a complex relationship, marked by both cooperation and controversy. This subchapter delves into the challenges and controversies that have shaped the political cooperation between these two nations.

One of the main challenges in Qatar-Iran political cooperation is the ongoing geopolitical rivalry in the Middle East. Qatar's close ties with Iran have often put it at odds with other regional powers, particularly Saudi Arabia and the United Arab Emirates. These countries have accused Qatar of supporting Iran and its regional proxies, leading to a strain in diplomatic relations.

Another challenge lies in the differences in political ideologies and systems between Qatar and Iran. While Qatar is a monarchy with a relatively liberal political environment, Iran is an Islamic Republic with a more conservative regime. These ideological differences have at times hindered the development of a seamless political cooperation between the two nations.

Controversies have also emerged in Qatar-Iran political cooperation, particularly in relation to Iran's involvement in conflicts in the region. Qatar has faced criticism for allegedly supporting Iran's proxies, such as Hezbollah and Hamas, which are deemed as terrorist organizations by some countries. These controversies have sparked tensions with other Gulf Cooperation Council (GCC) members who view Iran's activities as a threat to regional stability.

Moreover, Qatar's independent foreign policy and its diplomatic engagement with Iran have been met with skepticism and criticism from some quarters. While Qatar asserts that its engagement with Iran is aimed at promoting dialogue and resolving regional conflicts, critics argue that it risks undermining the collective efforts of the GCC and other international alliances.

Despite these challenges and controversies, Qatar and Iran have also found common ground in certain areas of political cooperation. Both countries have advocated for peaceful resolution of conflicts in the region, and have engaged in diplomatic efforts to mediate disputes. Additionally, they have collaborated in international fora, such as the

United Nations, to address shared concerns and promote stability in the region.

In conclusion, the political cooperation between Qatar and Iran is not without its challenges and controversies. The geopolitical rivalry, ideological differences, and controversies surrounding Iran's regional involvement have all posed hurdles to a seamless partnership. However, both nations have also demonstrated a willingness to engage in dialogue and find common ground, particularly in the pursuit of regional stability and conflict resolution.

The Role of Political Cooperation in Regional Security

In the ever-changing landscape of global politics, the role of political cooperation in ensuring regional security has become increasingly paramount. This subchapter delves into the importance of political cooperation between the State of Qatar and Iran in fostering stability and peace in the region. As diplomats, it is crucial to understand the nuances and dynamics of this cooperation, as well as its implications for various aspects such as trade, culture, energy, and security.

Qatar and Iran have long maintained a unique and intricate relationship, characterized by both cooperation and occasional tensions. It is within this context that political cooperation plays a pivotal role in enhancing regional security. By engaging in open and constructive dialogue, Qatar and Iran can address mutual concerns, resolve disputes, and promote peaceful coexistence. This cooperation serves as a vital mechanism to mitigate conflicts and prevent the escalation of tensions that could threaten the stability of the entire region.

One of the key areas where political cooperation between Qatar and Iran has proven instrumental is in the realm of security. Recognizing the shared interests in maintaining peace and stability, both nations have actively collaborated in counterterrorism efforts, intelligence sharing, and combating transnational threats. By combining their resources and expertise, Qatar and Iran have successfully thwarted attempts to destabilize the region, thereby safeguarding the interests of their respective countries and the broader Middle East.

Furthermore, political cooperation has facilitated increased collaboration in the fields of trade, culture, tourism, education, and energy. By fostering strong bilateral ties, Qatar and Iran have opened avenues for economic growth and cultural exchange. This interconnectedness not only strengthens the bond between the two nations but also contributes to the harmonious development of the region as a whole.

It is important to note that political cooperation does not imply a complete alignment of interests. Qatar and Iran may have divergent viewpoints on certain issues, but the ability to engage in constructive dialogue allows for the resolution of disagreements and the identification of common ground. This flexibility and willingness to cooperate despite differences are fundamental to maintaining stability and security in the region.

In conclusion, political cooperation plays a vital role in promoting regional security between Qatar and Iran. By embracing open dialogue, both nations can address shared concerns, enhance economic ties, and combat common threats. Through political cooperation, Qatar and Iran demonstrate their commitment to peace, stability, and the overall well-being of the Middle East. As diplomats, it is imperative to recognize and support the significance of such cooperation, as it paves the way for a brighter and more secure future for the entire region.

Chapter 7: Qatar-Iran Sports Diplomacy

The Power of Sports in Diplomatic Relations

Sports have long been recognized as a powerful tool for diplomacy and international relations. The State of Qatar has effectively harnessed the power of sports to bridge the gap and strengthen diplomatic ties with Iran, creating an open window to the world for the isolated nation.

Qatar and Iran, despite their differences, have found common ground in the realm of sports. The mutual love for sports, particularly football, has served as a catalyst for diplomatic relations between the two nations. Through various sporting events, Qatar and Iran have been able to foster a spirit of cooperation, understanding, and dialogue that extends beyond the playing field.

One of the most significant examples of sports diplomacy between Qatar and Iran is the Qatar Stars League. This professional football league has become a platform for cultural exchange and collaboration. Qatari and Iranian football clubs regularly compete against each other, creating an opportunity for players and fans from both nations to interact and develop a deeper understanding of one another's culture.

Furthermore, the State of Qatar has actively sought to host international sporting events that involve Iran. The hosting of the Asian Games and the AFC Asian Cup, for example, has provided a platform for athletes from both nations to compete and showcase their talents on an international stage. These events have not only strengthened the sporting ties between Qatar and Iran but have also allowed for cultural exchange and tourism between the two nations.

Sports diplomacy has also extended to other areas of cooperation between Qatar and Iran. The two nations have collaborated in the fields of education, academic research, and transport. This collaboration has facilitated the exchange of knowledge and ideas, promoting cultural understanding and strengthening diplomatic relations.

In conclusion, the power of sports in diplomatic relations cannot be underestimated. Qatar's efforts to utilize sports as a tool for diplomacy have not only bridged the gap between the State of Qatar and isolated Iran but have also opened a window to the world for the Iranian nation. Through sporting events and cultural exchanges, the two nations have been able to foster understanding, cooperation, and dialogue that extends beyond sports. Sports diplomacy has proven to be an effective means to strengthen diplomatic relations and build bridges between nations.

Qatar and Iran's Sporting Connections

Sports have long been recognized as a powerful tool for fostering diplomatic relations and building bridges between nations. In the case of Qatar and Iran, sports diplomacy has played a significant role in strengthening their bilateral ties and promoting mutual understanding. The sporting connections between these two nations encompass various disciplines, from football to equestrianism, and have contributed to the broader framework of Qatar-Iran diplomatic relations.

One of the most prominent examples of Qatar and Iran's sporting collaboration is their shared passion for football. Both countries have vibrant football cultures and have competed against each other in numerous international competitions. These matches not only provide an opportunity for friendly competition but also serve as a platform for cultural exchange and diplomacy. The Qatar-Iran football rivalry has brought together fans from both nations, fostering a sense of camaraderie and mutual respect.

Furthermore, Qatar and Iran have also engaged in joint initiatives to promote other sports, such as equestrianism. Qatar's world-renowned Al

Shaqab equestrian center has been a hub for international competitions and has attracted riders and enthusiasts from around the world, including Iran. This shared interest in equestrian sports has led to exchanges of knowledge and expertise between the two countries, further enhancing their sporting connections.

In addition to sports competitions, Qatar and Iran have also collaborated on hosting major sporting events. Qatar's successful bid to host the 2022 FIFA World Cup has provided an opportunity for closer cooperation between the two nations. Iran, being a regional powerhouse in football, has offered its support and expertise to Qatar in organizing this prestigious event. Such collaborations not only showcase the potential of sports diplomacy but also highlight the mutual trust and cooperation between Qatar and Iran.

Moreover, sports have also played a role in promoting cultural exchange and tourism between the two nations. Iran's rich cultural heritage has attracted many Qatari tourists, who have had the opportunity to witness Iran's sporting traditions firsthand. Likewise, Qatar's state-of-the-art sports facilities and world-class events have enticed Iranian visitors, fostering greater people-to-people connections.

In conclusion, Qatar and Iran's sporting connections have served as a catalyst for enhancing their bilateral relations. Through football, equestrianism, and joint hosting of major sporting events, the two nations have found common ground and built bridges of understanding. These sporting collaborations have not only strengthened diplomatic ties but also promoted cultural exchange, tourism, and people-to-people connections. As Qatar continues to serve as Iran's open window to the world, the role of sports diplomacy will undoubtedly remain a vital component of their multifaceted relationship.

Sporting Events as Platforms for Diplomacy

Sporting events have long served as platforms for diplomacy, providing opportunities for countries to engage in friendly competition, foster cultural exchange, and bridge political divides. The State of Qatar has recognized the potential of sports diplomacy, particularly in its relations with Iran, to strengthen diplomatic ties, promote economic cooperation, and enhance cultural understanding.

Qatar's engagement with Iran through sporting events has played a crucial role in opening a window to the world for the isolated nation. Despite political differences, Qatar has been able to forge a strong diplomatic bond with Iran through their shared love for sports. By hosting international tournaments such as the Asian Cup and the FIFA World Cup, Qatar has provided a platform for Iran to showcase its athletic prowess and engage in friendly competition with other nations.

This sporting diplomacy has not only strengthened Qatar-Iran diplomatic relations but has also facilitated increased trade and economic cooperation. The influx of visitors during major sporting events has provided opportunities for business networking and investment, boosting economic ties between the two nations. Qatar's strategic location and excellent infrastructure have made it an attractive destination for Iranian tourists, further promoting cultural exchange and tourism.

Furthermore, Qatar and Iran have collaborated in the field of energy, recognizing the mutual benefit of cooperation. Qatar, being a major exporter of liquefied natural gas (LNG), has engaged in energy cooperation with Iran, ensuring a stable supply of energy resources to meet both nations' growing demands.

In the political realm, Qatar and Iran have found common ground on various regional issues, forming alliances and cooperating to promote stability in the Gulf region. This collaboration has not only strengthened their bilateral relations but has also contributed to regional security and stability.

The State of Qatar has also been actively involved in promoting education and academic collaboration with Iran. Exchange programs, joint research projects, and scholarships have facilitated knowledge sharing and academic advancements, further fostering mutual understanding and cooperation.

Transport and connectivity have played a crucial role in enhancing Qatar-Iran relations. Improved air links, maritime connectivity, and initiatives such as the Qatar-Iran railway project have facilitated trade, tourism, and people-to-people exchanges, strengthening the bond between the two nations.

Additionally, Qatar has played a pivotal role in enhancing security cooperation with Iran, collaborating on counter-terrorism efforts, and jointly addressing regional security challenges. This strategic partnership has further bolstered Qatar-Iran relations and contributed to regional stability.

Lastly, media and information exchange have played a crucial role in promoting understanding and breaking down barriers between the two nations. Qatar's media outlets have provided a platform for Iranian perspectives, fostering dialogue and promoting cultural understanding.

In conclusion, sporting events have emerged as powerful tools for diplomacy, enabling Qatar and Iran to bridge the gap and establish a strong diplomatic relationship. Through sports diplomacy, the State of Qatar has successfully opened a window to the world for Iran, enabling the nation to engage globally and foster cooperation in various sectors including trade, tourism, energy, education, and security. This unique approach has not only benefited both nations but has also contributed to regional stability and understanding.

The Impact of Sports Diplomacy on Qatar-Iran Relations

Sports diplomacy has emerged as a powerful tool to foster international relations and enhance cultural exchanges between nations. In the context of Qatar-Iran relations, sports diplomacy has played a significant role in bridging the gap and strengthening ties between the two nations. This subchapter explores the impact of sports diplomacy on Qatar-Iran relations, highlighting how it has contributed to various aspects of their bilateral relationship.

Qatar and Iran, despite their geographical proximity, have had a complex and often strained relationship. However, sports diplomacy has served as a common ground for engagement and cooperation between the two nations. One of the most prominent examples of this is the FIFA World Cup 2022, which is set to be hosted by Qatar. The tournament has not only provided a platform for sporting excellence but has also acted as a catalyst for diplomatic engagement. Qatar's invitation to Iran to participate in the World Cup has fostered dialogue, collaboration, and mutual understanding between the nations.

Furthermore, sports diplomacy has had a positive impact on Qatar-Iran trade and economic relations. The hosting of major sporting events like the Asian Games and the Gulf Cup has attracted international investments and visitors to both countries. This has led to an increase in tourism and cultural exchange, creating new opportunities for business and trade between Qatar and Iran.

Sports diplomacy has also contributed to Qatar-Iran's cultural exchange and tourism sectors. Both nations have a rich cultural heritage, and through sports events, they have been able to showcase their traditions, customs, and hospitality. This has not only promoted cultural understanding but has also boosted tourism, as visitors are drawn to experience the unique cultural offerings of both countries.

Moreover, sports diplomacy has facilitated Qatar-Iran energy cooperation. Both nations are major players in the global energy market, and their collaboration in sports events has paved the way for dialogue on energy-related issues. Through sports diplomacy, the two countries have strengthened their energy ties and explored avenues for joint ventures and investment in the energy sector.

In addition, sports diplomacy has contributed to Qatar-Iran's political cooperation and alliances. The participation of Qatar and Iran in international sporting events has provided a platform for diplomatic engagement and dialogue on political issues of mutual concern. This has helped in building trust and fostering cooperation in various regional and international forums.

Furthermore, sports diplomacy has played a crucial role in Qatar-Iran's education and academic collaboration. Both nations have recognized the importance of sports as an educational tool and have promoted sports programs in their universities and educational institutions. This has facilitated student exchanges, research collaborations, and academic partnerships, leading to the exchange of knowledge and expertise in the field of sports.

In conclusion, sports diplomacy has had a profound impact on Qatar-Iran relations. It has acted as a catalyst for engagement and cooperation in various areas, including trade, culture, tourism, energy, politics, education, and more. By leveraging the power of sports, Qatar and Iran have been able to build bridges, foster understanding, and strengthen their bilateral relationship.

Chapter 8: Qatar-Iran Education and Academic Collaboration

The Importance of Education and Academic Exchange

In today's interconnected world, education and academic exchange play a vital role in fostering mutual understanding, cooperation, and development between nations. For the State of Qatar, education and academic collaboration with Iran hold immense significance as they serve as a gateway to bridging the gap between Qatar and the rest of the world. This subchapter explores the various aspects of Qatar-Iran education and academic exchange and highlights their importance in promoting diplomatic relations, trade and economic ties, cultural exchange, energy cooperation, political alliances, sports diplomacy, transport and connectivity, security cooperation, and media and information exchange.

Education serves as the foundation for the development of any nation. By investing in education and promoting academic exchange, Qatar and Iran can strengthen their diplomatic relations. Through educational initiatives such as student exchange programs, joint research projects, and faculty collaborations, both countries can foster cultural understanding, build trust, and establish long-lasting partnerships.

Qatar-Iran education and academic collaboration also have significant implications for trade and economic relations. By nurturing a skilled workforce through quality education, both countries can enhance their economic competitiveness and attract foreign investment. Furthermore, academic exchange can facilitate knowledge transfer, innovation, and entrepreneurship, leading to the development of new industries and job creation.

Cultural exchange and tourism are other crucial aspects of Qatar-Iran education and academic collaboration. By promoting the exchange of students, scholars, and cultural artifacts, both countries can showcase their rich heritage, traditions, and values. This cultural exchange will not only attract tourists but also foster a deeper appreciation for each other's culture, promoting mutual respect and understanding.

Energy cooperation between Qatar and Iran can be greatly enhanced through education and academic exchange. By sharing knowledge and expertise in the field of energy, both countries can develop sustainable solutions, optimize resource utilization, and strengthen their energy security.

Political cooperation and alliances can also be fostered through education and academic collaboration. By training future leaders, diplomats, and policymakers, both Qatar and Iran can build a network of professionals who understand each other's perspectives, enhancing their ability to work together on regional and global issues.

Qatar-Iran education and academic collaboration can also extend to sports diplomacy, transport and connectivity, security cooperation, and media and information exchange. By nurturing sports talents, promoting research in transportation and communication, sharing security expertise, and facilitating media collaborations, both countries can deepen their cooperation and strengthen their global presence.

In conclusion, education and academic exchange are essential for Qatar and Iran to bridge the gap and establish meaningful connections with the rest of the world. By prioritizing education, both countries can unlock numerous opportunities for diplomatic, economic, cultural, energy, political, sports, transport, security, and media cooperation. It is through education that Qatar and Iran can truly become open windows to the world.

Qatar and Iran's Educational Partnerships and Collaborations

Education plays a vital role in shaping a nation's future, fostering cross-cultural understanding, and strengthening diplomatic ties. In the case of Qatar and Iran, educational partnerships and collaborations have emerged as a key element in their efforts to bridge the gap and enhance mutual cooperation. This subchapter explores the various dimensions of Qatar and Iran's educational engagements, emphasizing the significance they hold for diplomats and the niches of State of Qatar: Isolated Iran's open window to the world, Qatar-Iran Diplomatic Relations, Qatar-Iran Trade and Economic Relations, Qatar-Iran Cultural Exchange and Tourism, Qatar-Iran Energy Cooperation, Qatar-Iran Political Cooperation and Alliances, Qatar-Iran Sports Diplomacy, Qatar-Iran Education and Academic Collaboration, Qatar-Iran Transport and Connectivity, Qatar-Iran Security Cooperation, and Qatar-Iran Media and Information Exchange.

Qatar and Iran have established strong academic partnerships, facilitating student and faculty exchanges, joint research initiatives, and the establishment of branch campuses. Qatar Foundation for Education, Science and Community Development has been at the forefront of these efforts, offering scholarships to Iranian students to pursue their higher education in Qatar. These initiatives not only contribute to the development of human capital in both countries but also foster cross-cultural dialogue and understanding.

Furthermore, Qatar and Iran have collaborated in the establishment of joint educational institutions. One notable example is the Qatar-Iran Joint Center for Islamic Studies, which promotes research and academic exchange in the field of Islamic studies. This center serves as a platform for scholars from both nations to engage in intellectual discourse and develop a deeper understanding of Islam's rich heritage.

In addition to academic collaborations, Qatar and Iran have also invested in cultural exchange programs and initiatives. These efforts aim to promote cultural understanding, heritage preservation, and tourism between the two nations. The Qatar Museums Authority has organized exhibitions showcasing Iranian art and history, further strengthening the cultural ties between the two countries.

The educational partnerships between Qatar and Iran extend beyond the academic realm. Collaborations in sports diplomacy have been witnessed through joint training programs, exchange of athletes, and organizing friendly matches. These initiatives not only promote sportsmanship but also serve as a platform to foster goodwill and strengthen people-to-people connections.

In conclusion, Qatar and Iran's educational partnerships and collaborations are essential components in their diplomatic relations. These initiatives contribute to bridging the gap between the two nations, promoting cross-cultural understanding, and building a strong foundation for future cooperation. By investing in education, both Qatar and Iran are not only nurturing their future leaders but also establishing long-lasting bonds of friendship and cooperation.

Joint Research Projects and Scholarly Exchanges

In the ever-evolving landscape of international relations, joint research projects and scholarly exchanges play a crucial role in fostering collaboration and understanding between nations. This subchapter explores the vibrant partnership between the State of Qatar and Iran in the realm of academia and research, highlighting the potential it holds for both countries in bridging the gap and promoting mutual growth.

Qatar and Iran have long recognized the significance of knowledge exchange in strengthening their diplomatic ties. By fostering collaborations between their respective universities and research institutions, both nations have been able to tap into a wealth of knowledge and expertise, creating a platform for meaningful academic dialogue and collaboration.

Through joint research projects, scholars and researchers from Qatar and Iran have had the opportunity to work together on cutting-edge research initiatives, tackling shared challenges, and making groundbreaking discoveries. These projects span various fields, including science, technology, medicine, social sciences, and humanities, harnessing the diverse strengths and resources of both nations.

Scholarly exchanges further enhance the academic partnership between Qatar and Iran. Through student and faculty exchange programs, researchers and scholars have the chance to immerse themselves in each other's educational systems, culture, and intellectual traditions. This not only deepens their understanding of each other's perspectives but also fosters long-lasting friendships and networks.

Moreover, these collaborations have a ripple effect on other aspects of Qatar-Iran relations. The knowledge gained and shared through joint research projects and scholarly exchanges can significantly impact the realms of trade, economics, culture, energy, politics, sports, education, transportation, security, and media between the two nations. It serves as a catalyst for further cooperation and collaboration in these sectors, ultimately strengthening the overall bilateral relationship.

For diplomats involved in Qatar-Iran relations, recognizing the potential of joint research projects and scholarly exchanges is of paramount importance. By supporting and facilitating such initiatives, diplomats can contribute to the growth and development of both nations, while also building bridges of understanding and cooperation.

In conclusion, joint research projects and scholarly exchanges have emerged as a powerful tool in fostering collaboration and understanding between the State of Qatar and Iran. By harnessing the collective knowledge and expertise of both nations, these initiatives have the potential to bridge the gap and open new windows of opportunity in various sectors. Diplomats must continue to prioritize and support these collaborations to ensure the sustained growth and development of Qatar-Iran relations.

The Role of Education in Strengthening Qatar-Iran Ties

Education has long been recognized as a powerful tool for bridging gaps and fostering understanding between nations. In the case of the State of Qatar and Iran, education plays a crucial role in strengthening diplomatic, cultural, economic, and political ties. This subchapter explores how education serves as a catalyst for collaboration and cooperation between Qatar and Iran.

Qatar and Iran share a common vision of promoting knowledge and fostering intellectual growth. Both nations understand the importance of investing in education to empower their citizens and drive economic development. Through educational exchanges and academic collaborations, Qatar and Iran have been able to nurture a strong foundation for their diplomatic relations.

The State of Qatar has opened its doors to Iranian students, providing them with world-class educational opportunities in its renowned universities. This not only enhances the academic experience of Iranian students but also creates a cultural exchange that promotes understanding and friendship between the two nations. Likewise, Qatari students have the opportunity to study in Iran, immersing themselves in its rich history and traditions.

The educational exchange between Qatar and Iran extends beyond the student community. Scholars and researchers from both countries engage in joint research projects, sharing their expertise and knowledge.

This collaboration has led to advancements in various fields, including science, technology, and medicine, benefiting both nations.

Furthermore, education acts as a catalyst for economic cooperation between Qatar and Iran. By investing in educational institutions and programs, both nations can develop a skilled workforce that meets the demands of their respective industries. This collaboration not only strengthens trade and economic relations but also opens doors for joint ventures and investment opportunities.

Education also plays a vital role in cultural exchange and tourism between Qatar and Iran. Through student exchange programs, cultural festivals, and language courses, both nations are able to foster a deeper appreciation and understanding of each other's heritage and traditions. This cultural exchange not only enriches the lives of the individuals involved but also promotes tourism between the two countries.

In the realm of politics, education serves as a platform for dialogue and cooperation. By promoting academic conferences, seminars, and workshops, Qatar and Iran can engage in meaningful discussions on regional and international issues. This intellectual exchange leads to a better understanding of each other's perspectives and strengthens their political cooperation and alliances.

In conclusion, education plays a multifaceted role in strengthening Qatar-Iran ties. Through educational exchanges, academic collaborations, and cultural programs, both nations are able to foster mutual understanding, enhance economic cooperation, and deepen their political alliances. By investing in education, Qatar and Iran have created an open window to the world, bridging the gap between them and promoting a brighter future for their diplomatic relations.

Chapter 9: Qatar-Iran Transport and Connectivity

Qatar and Iran's Transportation Infrastructure

Transportation plays a crucial role in connecting nations, fostering trade, and promoting cultural exchange. In the case of Qatar and Iran, their transportation infrastructure serves as a vital link that facilitates diplomatic, economic, and social cooperation between the two nations. This subchapter aims to shed light on the state of Qatar's efforts in bridging the gap with Iran through the enhancement of their transportation and connectivity.

Qatar, as a small peninsula in the Arabian Gulf, has invested significantly in developing its transportation system to strengthen its ties with Iran. The two countries are connected by air, land, and sea, providing multiple avenues for trade and human interaction. The Hamad International Airport in Doha serves as a major hub for connecting flights to various cities in Iran, making it convenient for diplomats, businessmen, and tourists to travel between the two nations.

Furthermore, Qatar's expansive seaports, such as the Port of Doha and the Port of Ras Laffan, serve as major gateways for maritime trade with Iran. These ports facilitate the transportation of goods, including energy resources, between the two countries. The completion of the Qatar-Iran gas pipeline has further enhanced their energy cooperation, ensuring a steady supply of gas to Iran and boosting their economic relations.

In recent years, Qatar has also focused on improving its land transportation infrastructure to enhance connectivity with Iran. The development of the Qatar-Iran Friendship Bridge, also known as the Sheikh Jassim Bin Hamad Bridge, is a testament to this commitment. Once completed, this bridge will provide a direct road link between

Qatar and Iran, facilitating the movement of goods and people, and fostering closer ties between the two nations.

Moreover, Qatar's transportation initiatives extend beyond infrastructure development. The country has actively engaged in joint ventures with Iran in the airline industry, with Qatar Airways offering regular flights to major cities in Iran. This collaboration not only boosts tourism but also enhances cultural exchange and people-to-people connections.

In conclusion, Qatar's efforts in improving its transportation infrastructure have been instrumental in bridging the gap with Iran. These initiatives have not only strengthened their diplomatic and economic relations but have also promoted cultural exchange, tourism, and academic collaboration. As Qatar continues to invest in the development of its transportation and connectivity with Iran, it paves the way for a closer and more mutually beneficial relationship between the two nations.

Enhancing Connectivity through Transportation Projects

Transportation plays a crucial role in enhancing connectivity between nations, fostering economic growth, and strengthening diplomatic relations. In the State of Qatar, transportation projects have become a cornerstone of the country's efforts to bridge gaps and establish itself as Iran's open window to the world. This subchapter explores the various transportation initiatives undertaken by Qatar to improve connectivity with Iran and the wider region.

One of the key transportation projects is the development of a robust road network between Qatar and Iran. This project aims to facilitate the movement of people and goods, promoting trade and economic relations between the two nations. The construction of highways and bridges has not only enhanced connectivity but also reduced travel time significantly, making it easier for diplomats and businesspeople to travel between Qatar and Iran.

In addition to roads, Qatar has also invested in expanding its air connectivity with Iran. The State-owned Qatar Airways has increased the number of flights to Iranian cities, providing more options for diplomats and tourists alike. This increase in air connectivity has not only facilitated travel but has also strengthened Qatar-Iran diplomatic relations, as it enables more frequent exchanges between officials from both countries.

Furthermore, Qatar's focus on enhancing connectivity extends to maritime transportation as well. The State of Qatar has heavily invested in expanding its port infrastructure, including the development of the Hamad Port, which has become a major hub for trade and transshipment. This port serves as a key gateway for goods entering and exiting Iran, further promoting trade and economic relations between the two nations.

In addition to physical connectivity, Qatar has also emphasized the importance of digital connectivity. The country has invested in state-of-the-art telecommunications infrastructure, ensuring high-speed internet connectivity and seamless communication between Qatar and Iran. This digital connectivity not only facilitates information exchange but also supports Qatar-Iran media collaborations, academic collaborations, and cultural exchanges.

By enhancing transportation projects, Qatar has successfully positioned itself as Iran's open window to the world. These projects have not only fostered economic growth and strengthened trade relations but have also promoted cultural exchange, tourism, and academic collaborations. As diplomats, it is crucial to recognize the significance of transportation in shaping diplomatic relations and to leverage these initiatives to further enhance Qatar-Iran diplomatic ties.

Challenges and Opportunities in Qatar-Iran Transport Cooperation

Transportation is a crucial aspect of international relations, facilitating the movement of people, goods, and ideas between nations. In the case of Qatar and Iran, a deep understanding of the challenges and opportunities in their transport cooperation is essential for diplomats and stakeholders involved in strengthening their bilateral relations. This subchapter explores the various aspects of Qatar-Iran transport cooperation and the potential it holds for both nations.

One of the primary challenges in Qatar-Iran transport cooperation is the geographical distance between the two countries. Qatar, located on the Arabian Peninsula, and Iran, spanning across Southwest Asia, are separated by the Persian Gulf. The vast expanse of water poses logistical difficulties in terms of establishing direct transportation links. However, with the advancement of technology and infrastructure, this challenge can be overcome through the development of efficient maritime routes and airline connections.

Another obstacle to Qatar-Iran transport cooperation is the ongoing political tensions in the region. The complex geopolitical landscape, including conflicts and rivalries, can hinder the smooth flow of transportation between the two countries. Diplomatic efforts are necessary to address these challenges and create an atmosphere conducive to enhanced transport cooperation.

Despite these challenges, numerous opportunities exist for Qatar and Iran to further strengthen their transport cooperation. One such opportunity lies in the expansion of air travel between the two countries. Qatar Airways, the national carrier of Qatar, already operates flights to major Iranian cities, providing convenient access for travelers. By increasing flight frequencies and exploring new routes, air transport can become a vital link between Qatar and Iran, promoting tourism, trade, and cultural exchange.

Additionally, the development of maritime infrastructure and trade routes can significantly boost Qatar-Iran transport cooperation. The strategic location of Qatar's ports, combined with Iran's extensive coastline along the Persian Gulf, provides an excellent opportunity for the establishment of maritime trade corridors. Strengthening port infrastructure, simplifying customs procedures, and promoting maritime cooperation can enhance bilateral trade and economic relations.

Furthermore, the construction of a land connection between Qatar and Iran holds immense potential. Currently, the only overland route between the two countries is through Saudi Arabia, which poses challenges due to political tensions. Exploring alternative land routes, such as through Oman or Iraq, can provide a direct and secure passage for goods and people, fostering closer ties between Qatar and Iran.

In conclusion, while challenges exist in Qatar-Iran transport cooperation, there are numerous opportunities to overcome them. By expanding air travel, developing maritime infrastructure, and exploring alternative land routes, Qatar and Iran can enhance their bilateral relations, promote trade and economic cooperation, and foster cultural exchange and tourism. Diplomats and stakeholders must work together to address these challenges and seize the opportunities that transport cooperation brings for both nations.

The Role of Transport in Facilitating Trade and People-to-People Contact

Transport plays a crucial role in facilitating trade and people-to-people contact between nations. In the case of Qatar and Iran, transport has been instrumental in bridging the gap and strengthening their diplomatic, economic, cultural, and political ties. This subchapter explores the significance of transport in fostering connectivity and cooperation between the State of Qatar and Iran.

Qatar has long been considered Iran's open window to the world, and transport has been the key to unlocking this window. With direct air links between Doha and major Iranian cities, such as Tehran and Mashhad, people from both nations have been able to easily travel and establish personal connections. This has fostered cultural exchange, tourism, and educational collaborations, allowing individuals to experience each other's traditions, heritage, and way of life.

Moreover, transport infrastructure has played a vital role in boosting trade and economic relations between Qatar and Iran. Maritime transport has facilitated the movement of goods and commodities, enabling the exchange of resources and promoting economic growth. Qatar's strategic location as a maritime hub has provided a gateway for Iranian exports to reach international markets and vice versa. Additionally, the Qatar-Iran Gas Pipeline has further enhanced bilateral economic ties, ensuring a steady supply of natural gas from Iran to Qatar.

Transport has also been instrumental in strengthening political alliances and security cooperation between Qatar and Iran. Regular diplomatic visits and high-level meetings have been made possible through efficient air connectivity, allowing officials to discuss mutual concerns, coordinate policies, and foster diplomatic relations. Furthermore, transport infrastructure has facilitated collaboration in the field of security, enabling intelligence sharing, joint military exercises, and counterterrorism efforts.

In the realm of media and information exchange, transport has played a crucial role in ensuring the flow of news and communication. The establishment of direct satellite links between Qatar and Iran has allowed for the exchange of information, cultural programs, and news broadcasts, enhancing mutual understanding and promoting accurate reporting.

In conclusion, transport has emerged as a vital component in bridging the gap between Qatar and Iran. By facilitating trade, people-to-people contact, cultural exchange, and political cooperation, transport has contributed significantly to strengthening their diplomatic, economic, and cultural ties. As both nations continue to invest in transport infrastructure and connectivity, the future holds even greater potential for collaboration and cooperation in various sectors.

Chapter 10: Qatar-Iran Security Cooperation

The Importance of Security Cooperation in the Gulf Region

In the ever-evolving landscape of international relations, security cooperation plays a pivotal role, particularly in regions like the Gulf. The State of Qatar recognizes the significance of fostering security cooperation in the Gulf region, and this subchapter aims to shed light on its importance.

The Gulf region is known for its geopolitical complexities, with various political, economic, and social challenges. In this context, security cooperation becomes crucial to ensure stability, peace, and prosperity for all nations involved. The State of Qatar, in particular, has consistently prioritized security cooperation within the Gulf region, recognizing that a secure and stable neighborhood is vital for its own progress and development.

One of the key reasons for emphasizing security cooperation is the threat of terrorism and extremism that looms over the Gulf region. By collaborating closely with neighboring countries and international partners, the State of Qatar aims to combat these threats effectively. Sharing intelligence, conducting joint military exercises, and coordinating counter-terrorism efforts are essential components of such cooperation. By working together, the Gulf nations can effectively neutralize the elements that seek to undermine peace and stability.

Moreover, security cooperation in the Gulf region is not limited to counter-terrorism measures. It extends to maritime security, border control, and cybersecurity as well. Given the strategic location of the Gulf, protecting maritime routes, ensuring the safety of shipping lanes, and preventing illicit activities such as piracy and smuggling are crucial for the region's economic vitality. By cooperating on these fronts, the Gulf nations can collectively safeguard their interests and promote regional prosperity.

Furthermore, security cooperation serves as a foundation for building trust and fostering diplomatic relations among nations. By engaging in joint military exercises, intelligence sharing, and defense agreements, the Gulf states can strengthen their relationships and build a sense of camaraderie. This trust and cooperation can extend beyond security matters and serve as a catalyst for collaboration in other areas such as trade, economics, culture, education, and sports.

The State of Qatar recognizes that security cooperation is not a one-size-fits-all approach but requires tailored strategies and partnerships. By actively engaging in initiatives such as the Gulf Cooperation Council (GCC), the State of Qatar demonstrates its commitment to regional security and stability. Through such platforms, the Gulf nations can address common challenges collectively, exchange best practices, and develop comprehensive security frameworks.

In conclusion, security cooperation in the Gulf region is of paramount importance. The State of Qatar acknowledges this significance and actively engages in various initiatives and partnerships to promote regional stability and prosperity. By prioritizing security cooperation, the Gulf nations can effectively address common threats, build trust, and lay the groundwork for broader diplomatic, economic, and cultural collaborations.

Qatar and Iran's Shared Security Concerns

In recent years, Qatar and Iran have found themselves facing similar security challenges, which have fostered a shared understanding and collaboration in the realm of security cooperation. This subchapter explores the various aspects of Qatar and Iran's shared security concerns and how they have worked together to address these issues.

Both Qatar and Iran have found themselves isolated from the international community due to various geopolitical reasons. Qatar has faced a regional blockade by its neighboring countries, while Iran has been subject to economic sanctions imposed by Western powers. These shared experiences of isolation have brought the two nations closer, prompting them to seek mutual support and cooperation.

One of the primary security concerns shared by Qatar and Iran is the threat of terrorism and extremism in the region. Both countries have been targeted by terrorist organizations and share a common goal of countering these threats. Qatar and Iran have strengthened their intelligence sharing and coordination efforts to combat terrorism and ensure the safety of their respective nations.

Another area of shared concern is the stability of the Gulf region. Qatar and Iran understand the importance of maintaining peace and stability in the region for their own security and economic interests. They have engaged in diplomatic dialogues and negotiations to find peaceful resolutions to regional conflicts and have advocated for dialogue-based approaches rather than resorting to military interventions.

Qatar and Iran have also developed strong economic ties, which further enhances their shared security concerns. Both countries heavily rely on energy exports, and any disruptions in the global energy market can have severe repercussions on their economies. As a result, Qatar and Iran have collaborated on energy policies, including the establishment of joint ventures and investments in the energy sector, to ensure stability and security in the region.

Furthermore, Qatar and Iran have recognized the importance of cultural exchange and tourism in fostering understanding and building bridges between nations. They have promoted cultural events, organized exchange programs, and facilitated tourism between their countries. By encouraging people-to-people interactions, Qatar and Iran aim to enhance mutual understanding and contribute to regional stability and security.

In conclusion, Qatar and Iran share common security concerns that have brought them closer together. From countering terrorism to promoting regional stability and economic cooperation, the two nations have collaborated on various fronts. By addressing these shared concerns, Qatar and Iran are not only ensuring their own security but also contributing to the overall stability and peace in the region.

Joint Military Exercises and Cooperation

In the realm of international diplomacy, military exercises and cooperation play a vital role in fostering trust, strengthening alliances, and maintaining regional security. This subchapter will delve into the joint military exercises and cooperation between the State of Qatar and Iran, shedding light on the various dimensions and objectives of this strategic partnership.

The State of Qatar and Iran have recognized the significance of military collaboration in promoting stability and countering potential threats. Both nations have engaged in joint military exercises to enhance their defense capabilities and establish a robust deterrent against common adversaries. These exercises serve as a platform for sharing technical expertise, exchanging best practices, and improving interoperability between their armed forces.

The joint military exercises between Qatar and Iran also bolster their diplomatic relations. By engaging in military cooperation, both nations demonstrate their commitment to regional security and their determination to work together in addressing common challenges. These exercises serve as a tangible symbol of the trust and confidence that exist between the two countries, fostering a sense of unity and solidarity.

Furthermore, Qatar and Iran have realized the economic advantages of military cooperation. These joint exercises create opportunities for defense industries in both nations, stimulating economic growth and job creation. The exchange of military technologies and equipment can enhance the domestic defense capabilities of both countries, reducing their dependence on foreign suppliers and boosting their respective defense sectors.

The joint military exercises and cooperation also extend to capacity-building initiatives, such as training programs and knowledge exchange. Qatar and Iran collaborate in educating their military personnel, equipping them with the necessary skills and knowledge to effectively respond to evolving security threats. This collaboration in military education fosters a deeper understanding between the armed forces of both nations and enhances their ability to work together seamlessly in future operations.

In conclusion, joint military exercises and cooperation between the State of Qatar and Iran serve as a crucial pillar of their bilateral relations. By fostering trust, enhancing defense capabilities, and promoting economic growth, these exercises contribute to regional stability and security. The strategic partnership between Qatar and Iran in the military domain demonstrates their shared commitment to peace and prosperity in the region.

The Role of Security Cooperation in Regional Stability

In today's complex and interconnected world, regional stability is of utmost importance for the progress and prosperity of nations. As the State of Qatar continues to strengthen its diplomatic ties with Iran, it recognizes the vital role that security cooperation plays in maintaining peace and stability in the region. This subchapter delves into the significance of security cooperation in fostering regional stability between Qatar and Iran.

Qatar and Iran share a common goal of ensuring the security and stability of the Arabian Gulf region. By working together on security matters, these two nations can effectively address common challenges such as terrorism, maritime security, and border control. Security cooperation serves as a foundation for building trust and understanding between Qatar and Iran, paving the way for enhanced diplomatic relations.

The State of Qatar has been actively engaged in combatting terrorism and extremism on a global scale. By collaborating with Iran in the field of security, Qatar can further contribute to the collective efforts in eradicating this menace. Intelligence sharing, joint training programs, and coordinated border control measures are some of the ways in which security cooperation can effectively combat the threats posed by terrorist organizations.

Moreover, security cooperation between Qatar and Iran extends beyond addressing traditional security concerns. It also encompasses cyber security, energy security, and the protection of critical infrastructure. By sharing expertise, best practices, and technological advancements, both nations can fortify their defenses against emerging threats in these domains.

Furthermore, security cooperation plays a crucial role in facilitating economic growth and development. A secure and stable environment is essential for trade and investment to flourish between Qatar and Iran. By jointly addressing security challenges, both nations can create a conducive atmosphere for businesses to thrive, thereby boosting bilateral trade and economic relations.

In conclusion, security cooperation is pivotal in maintaining regional stability between Qatar and Iran. By collaborating on security matters, both nations can effectively combat terrorism, enhance border control measures, and protect critical infrastructure. This cooperation not only strengthens diplomatic ties but also fosters economic growth and development. As Qatar and Iran continue to engage in security cooperation, they contribute to a safer and more prosperous region for all.

Chapter 11: Qatar-Iran Media and Information Exchange

The Power of Media in Shaping Perceptions and Narratives

In today's interconnected world, media plays a crucial role in shaping perceptions and narratives. It has the power to influence public opinion, create awareness, and ultimately shape the way we see the world. This subchapter explores the impact of media in bridging the gap between the State of Qatar and Iran, highlighting its influence in various aspects of diplomatic, economic, cultural, and political cooperation.

The media serves as a powerful tool in shaping the narrative around the State of Qatar's relationship with Iran. It provides a platform for diplomats to communicate their perspectives, share information, and engage in dialogue. Through media channels, diplomats can address misconceptions, correct inaccuracies, and foster a deeper understanding of the dynamics between the two countries.

Moreover, media acts as a bridge between Qatar and Iran, facilitating communication and exchange in various sectors. It plays a pivotal role in promoting economic relations by showcasing investment opportunities, trade agreements, and joint ventures. Through media coverage, diplomats can highlight the benefits of Qatar-Iran economic cooperation, encouraging businesses to explore new horizons and strengthen bilateral ties.

Cultural exchange and tourism are also areas where media plays a vital role. By showcasing the rich cultural heritage, traditions, and tourist attractions of both countries, media fosters a sense of curiosity and interest. Through documentaries, travel shows, and social media platforms, diplomats can promote Qatar-Iran cultural exchange, encouraging people to explore the diverse landscapes, historical sites, and vibrant communities.

Media's influence extends to the energy sector, where it serves as a platform to highlight Qatar-Iran energy cooperation. Through interviews, articles, and conferences, diplomats can emphasize the significance of collaboration in this crucial sector. By showcasing joint projects, technological advancements, and sustainable practices, media plays a vital role in driving energy cooperation between Qatar and Iran.

Political cooperation and alliances are also shaped by media narratives. Diplomats can leverage media platforms to highlight common interests, shared values, and collaborative efforts in addressing regional challenges. By fostering a positive perception through media channels, diplomats can build trust and strengthen Qatar-Iran political cooperation.

In the realm of sports diplomacy, media acts as a catalyst for promoting Qatar-Iran sporting events and collaborations. Through coverage of tournaments, interviews with athletes, and documentaries, media fosters a spirit of sportsmanship, unity, and friendship.

Furthermore, media plays a crucial role in promoting educational and academic collaboration between Qatar and Iran. By highlighting student exchange programs, joint research projects, and academic conferences, diplomats can encourage young minds to engage in cross-cultural learning and knowledge-sharing.

Media also plays a vital role in enhancing transport and connectivity between Qatar and Iran. By showcasing infrastructure projects, air routes, and maritime collaborations, diplomats can highlight the ease of travel and trade between the two nations.

Lastly, media contributes to Qatar-Iran security cooperation by disseminating information on joint efforts in combating terrorism, preserving regional stability, and ensuring the safety of both countries.

In conclusion, the power of media in shaping perceptions and narratives cannot be underestimated. It plays a pivotal role in promoting dialogue, fostering understanding, and building bridges between the State of Qatar and Iran. Through media channels, diplomats can leverage its potential to strengthen diplomatic, economic, cultural, and political cooperation, ultimately bridging the gap and creating a more interconnected world.

Qatar and Iran's Media Landscape

In the ever-evolving world of media and information exchange, Qatar and Iran have played significant roles in shaping the narrative and promoting their respective agendas. This subchapter aims to explore the dynamic media landscapes of both countries and the impact they have on the broader diplomatic relations between Qatar and Iran.

Qatar, often regarded as a regional media powerhouse, has made significant investments in its media industry, particularly with the establishment of Al Jazeera. This influential news network has revolutionized the Arab media landscape by providing a platform for alternative voices and perspectives. Al Jazeera has played a crucial role in shaping public opinion, not only in Qatar but also in the wider Arab world, including Iran. Its coverage of regional conflicts, political developments, and social issues has often challenged the status quo and provided a platform for marginalized voices.

Similarly, Iran boasts a diverse and vibrant media landscape, albeit with more restrictions compared to Qatar. State-controlled media outlets like Press TV and Islamic Republic of Iran Broadcasting (IRIB) serve as the primary sources of news and information within Iran. These outlets, often aligned with the government's narrative, play a crucial role in shaping public opinion and promoting Iran's political and ideological agenda. However, despite such restrictions, Iran has witnessed the emergence of alternative media platforms, particularly on social media, which have allowed for a more diverse range of voices and perspectives to be heard.

The media landscape of Qatar and Iran has a significant impact on their diplomatic relations. Through media and information exchange, both countries have sought to project their soft power and influence regional dynamics. The media serves as a tool for public diplomacy, allowing governments to shape public perception and garner support for their policies and initiatives.

Furthermore, media collaboration between Qatar and Iran has expanded in recent years, particularly in the realm of cultural exchange. Both countries have facilitated the exchange of films, television programs, and documentaries, showcasing their respective cultural heritage and fostering a deeper understanding between their peoples.

In conclusion, the media landscapes of Qatar and Iran play a crucial role in shaping public opinion, promoting their respective agendas, and influencing diplomatic relations. Qatar's Al Jazeera and Iran's state-controlled media outlets have served as powerful tools in projecting their soft power and shaping regional dynamics. Moreover, media collaboration and cultural exchange between the two countries have fostered a greater understanding and appreciation of each other's cultural heritage. As the media landscape continues to evolve, it will undoubtedly play a vital role in shaping the future of Qatar-Iran relations and the broader regional dynamics.

Collaborative Media Projects and Exchanges

In today's interconnected world, media plays a crucial role in shaping diplomatic relations and promoting cultural understanding between nations. Collaborative media projects and exchanges between countries have become increasingly important in fostering dialogue, promoting cultural exchange, and bridging gaps between nations. This subchapter explores the significance of such projects and exchanges in the context of Qatar and Iran, shedding light on how they contribute to the relationship between the two countries.

Qatar and Iran share a unique relationship, characterized by a rich history and cultural ties. Collaborative media projects and exchanges serve as a powerful tool to enhance this relationship further. Through joint productions, documentaries, and news exchanges, both countries can showcase their respective cultures, traditions, and values to a global audience. These projects not only contribute to a more accurate and nuanced understanding of the State of Qatar and Iran but also help dispel misconceptions and stereotypes.

The media serves as a bridge between nations, enabling the exchange of ideas and knowledge. Collaborative media projects and exchanges facilitate cultural exchange and tourism between Qatar and Iran. By promoting each other's tourist attractions, historical sites, and cultural events, both countries can attract more visitors and boost their tourism sectors. This, in turn, has a positive impact on the economy, creating opportunities for investment and trade.

Furthermore, media collaborations foster educational and academic collaboration between Qatar and Iran. By sharing research, organizing joint conferences, and facilitating student exchanges, both countries can enhance their academic institutions' capabilities. This exchange of knowledge contributes to the development of a skilled workforce and promotes innovation.

Collaborative media projects and exchanges also play a crucial role in promoting political, economic, and security cooperation between Qatar and Iran. By sharing information and insights, both countries can strengthen their alliances and work towards common goals. The media acts as a platform for open dialogue, allowing for the exchange of views and opinions on various political and security matters.

In conclusion, collaborative media projects and exchanges have the power to shape diplomatic relations and promote cultural understanding between nations. In the case of Qatar and Iran, these initiatives serve as a means to bridge the gap and foster a stronger relationship. By showcasing each other's cultures, traditions, and values, promoting tourism and education, and facilitating political and security cooperation, media collaborations contribute to a more prosperous and interconnected world.

The Role of Media in Enhancing Understanding and Communication

In the modern globalized world, media plays a crucial role in enhancing understanding and communication between nations. This subchapter explores the significant impact of media in bridging the gap between the State of Qatar and Iran, facilitating diplomatic relations, trade and economic cooperation, cultural exchange, and more.

In the realm of diplomacy, media acts as a powerful tool for diplomats to communicate with each other and with the public. Through various media channels, diplomats can convey their messages, share information, and express their countries' positions on different issues. In the context of the State of Qatar and Iran, media serves as a platform for diplomatic discussions, enabling both nations to address concerns, resolve conflicts, and strengthen bilateral ties.

Furthermore, media plays a pivotal role in fostering trade and economic relations between the two nations. By promoting Qatar-Iran trade opportunities, media outlets facilitate the exchange of goods and services, attracting foreign investments and boosting economic growth. Through informative reports, articles, and interviews, media provides valuable insights into the business environment, investment opportunities, and economic policies of both countries, encouraging cross-border collaborations and partnerships.

Cultural exchange and tourism are also greatly enhanced by media. Through documentaries, travel shows, online platforms, and social media, media outlets highlight the rich cultural heritage, tourist attractions, and traditions of both Qatar and Iran. This exposure not only promotes tourism but also fosters a deeper understanding and appreciation of each other's cultures, breaking down stereotypes and building bridges between the two nations.

Media also plays a vital role in the energy sector, facilitating Qatar-Iran energy cooperation. Through news reports, interviews, and analysis, media outlets inform the public about energy-related developments, projects, and collaborations between the two countries. This information sharing helps in building trust and transparency, ensuring the smooth functioning of energy agreements and partnerships.

Furthermore, media acts as a platform for political cooperation and alliances between Qatar and Iran. By reporting on political developments, policy changes, and diplomatic initiatives, media keeps the public informed about the ongoing collaborations and strategic alliances between the two nations. This transparency fosters trust and understanding, strengthening the foundations of political cooperation.

Media also contributes to sports diplomacy, education and academic collaboration, transport and connectivity, security cooperation, and information exchange between Qatar and Iran. Through comprehensive coverage of sports events, educational programs, transportation projects, security initiatives, and news updates, media outlets facilitate understanding, collaboration, and cooperation in these various domains.

In conclusion, media plays a pivotal role in enhancing understanding and communication between the State of Qatar and Iran. Through its diverse channels and platforms, media acts as a catalyst for diplomatic relations, trade and economic cooperation, cultural exchange, energy cooperation, political alliances, sports diplomacy, education, and security cooperation. By promoting dialogue, sharing information, and fostering a deeper understanding, media bridges the gap between these two nations, creating a stronger and more interconnected Qatar-Iran relationship.

Note: The sub-chapters can be further expanded into more detailed sections or sub-sections as needed.

Qatar, a small but influential nation in the Middle East, has played a crucial role in bridging the gap between Iran and the rest of the world. This subchapter aims to provide an overview of the various aspects that contribute to the State of Qatar being Iran's open window to the world. In this subchapter, we will explore the diplomatic, economic, cultural, energy, political, sports, education, transport, security, and media aspects of Qatar's relationship with Iran.

Diplomats from around the world have recognized Qatar as a key player in facilitating dialogue and negotiations between Iran and other nations. Qatar's diplomatic efforts have helped ease tensions and promote understanding between Iran and the international community. The State of Qatar has also played a significant role in mediating conflicts in the region, further solidifying its position as a bridge between Iran and the rest of the world.

Qatar-Iran diplomatic relations have been robust, with both countries sharing common interests in regional stability and economic development. The two nations have engaged in regular high-level meetings and have signed various agreements to enhance cooperation in areas such as trade, investment, and defense.

The trade and economic relations between Qatar and Iran have flourished over the years. Qatar has become an important trading partner for Iran, importing various goods and services, while also investing in Iran's economy. The State of Qatar has also facilitated the establishment of joint ventures and encouraged bilateral trade between the two nations.

Cultural exchange and tourism have played a vital role in strengthening the relationship between Qatar and Iran. The two countries have embraced each other's cultural heritage and promoted tourism between their nations. Qatar has hosted Iranian cultural events and exhibitions, fostering a deeper understanding and appreciation of Iranian culture among its citizens.

Energy cooperation between Qatar and Iran has been significant, with both countries being major players in the global energy market. Qatar has invested in Iran's oil and gas sector, contributing to its development and enhancing energy security in the region. The two nations have also collaborated on joint energy projects, further cementing their partnership.

Qatar and Iran have shared political cooperation and alliances on various regional and international issues. They have collaborated on matters such as regional security, counter-terrorism, and conflict resolution, working together to promote stability in the Middle East.

Sports diplomacy has played a unique role in Qatar-Iran relations, with both countries participating in various sporting events and competitions. Qatar has hosted Iranian sports teams, fostering goodwill and enhancing people-to-people exchanges between the two nations.

Education and academic collaboration have been instrumental in promoting knowledge-sharing and intellectual exchange between Qatar and Iran. Universities and academic institutions in both countries have engaged in student and faculty exchanges, research collaborations, and joint academic programs, contributing to the development of human capital in both nations.

Transport and connectivity have been key areas of cooperation between Qatar and Iran. Qatar Airways operates regular flights to various cities in Iran, facilitating travel and trade between the two countries. Qatar has also invested in infrastructure projects in Iran, improving connectivity and transportation networks.

Security cooperation between Qatar and Iran has focused on counter-terrorism, border security, and defense collaboration. The two nations have worked closely to address common security challenges and enhance regional stability.

Lastly, media and information exchange have played a crucial role in promoting understanding and awareness between Qatar and Iran. Both countries have encouraged media cooperation, allowing for the exchange of news, information, and cultural content, further strengthening their relationship.

In conclusion, the State of Qatar has played a pivotal role in bridging the gap between Iran and the rest of the world. Through diplomatic, economic, cultural, energy, political, sports, education, transport, security, and media cooperation, Qatar has facilitated dialogue, understanding, and collaboration between Iran and the international community. The relationship between Qatar and Iran continues to evolve and flourish, with both nations recognizing the mutual benefits of their partnership.

www.ingramcontent.com/pod-product-compliance
Lightning Source LLC
Chambersburg PA
CBHW051242160726
47994CB00002B/984